Free to Be Creative at the Piano

A Revolutionary Approach to Music Making

EDWARD WEISS

Published by Quiescence Music

Table of Contents

Composition

A Quick and Easy Composition Method

Here's the method I use every time I want to capture an idea. I draw out 8-bars (or measures) first. Why eight bars? Because it is an ideal framework to work in. Eight bars of music are enough to generate a complete musical sentence and can usually be repeated once or twice. Next, I improvise and see what comes up. THEN, I will write down the chords I am playing and the first 2-bars of melody.

Writing down the first 2-bars of melody helps me remember the entire theme for the 8-bar phrase. I usually stay within one key to make it easy. This means I'll have 6 chords to work with. In C Major, the chords would be, C Maj. -D min. -E min. -F Maj. -G Maj. and A min. This is more than enough material to work with. In fact, I rarely use more than 3 or 4 chords for the first 8-bars.

Once you get your first 8-bars down, you're more than halfway home. Why? Because you already have the beginning. The rest of the piece, if there is a rest of the piece, can be finished by drawing more bar lines AND LISTENING FOR THE NEXT SECTION OF MUSIC. This is always accomplished through improvisation.

Your best material will ALWAYS come from improvisation because you are not thinking about creating something.

Instead, you are allowing the music that is inside of you to come to the surface without forcing it or willing it into being. You use the 8-bar framework to hold your ideas.

There is no rule that says you must work within 8-bars. You can use four or even sixteen bar phrases, however, its good to be able to feel the form and structure of an 8-bar phrase first. It is the structure used by most composers and it is wise to understand it.

Beautiful Music - Create It Yourself with New Age Piano

You've heard it many times before. Perhaps while you were out shopping or at a friends house. The beautiful music that has become known as New Age piano was first popularized by pianist/composer George Winston in the early 1980's.

Light and heartfelt, the melodies and chords of this piano style are not difficult to create. It's an attractive way for the beginning AND more advanced piano player to get started in music making! Let's examine how a complete beginner can create a lovely melody using just a few chords.

First, we must learn how to play chords on the piano. Note reading won't do here because we're trying to create something original -something that requires the ability to improvise. Now don't get scared! Improvisation is a lot easier than you think and you can produce beautiful music with just a few chords.

For example, in the lesson "Reflections in Water," available below, we use just 4 chords to create a calm, reflective atmosphere. The trick is how the chords are used! Both hands are called into play as we create a modern sounding open position seventh chord - the kind of chord that is used in much contemporary music created today.

We learn how to play just four chords in this lesson, but four chords are all we need to produce a few minutes of improvised music. Once you have this large chord structure under your fingers, beautiful music is created; not by forcing or willing the creative act, but BY ALLOWING IT TO HAPPEN!

We take our time and play around with this chord structure and marvel at how easy it is to create music with it. It's not difficult. It's not hard. It can be a little scary to jump in and begin improvising but once you taste how wonderful the water is, you'll jump in and have a hard time coming out!

Compose Music the Easy Way!

There are basically two ways to compose music. One way is by starting from the bottom or the harmonic approach.

A composer/arranger takes a few chords, a phrase to hang them on and arranges the harmony in some kind of pattern. An example of this is the "loop" you often hear in contemporary music. A loop is simply a harmonic background over which a melody (or not) is played.

The second way to compose music is by starting with the melody. Composers may or may not have some idea of the finished idea (I prefer not to) but the melodic idea is fitted into some kind of phrase. The most common phrase used is the 8-bar phrase.

<u>I find that starting with the melody to be the easier approach.</u> Why? Because melody is easier to move forward then harmony. Sure, you can block out a few chords and arrange them to create a loop, but this becomes static over time. Melody is much easier to go forward with.

By using the principles of repetition and contrast, we can create a simple ABA form in no time at all. Then we can go back and harmonize each section.

I used to favor the harmonic approach at first. It was very easy to simply jot down chord changes on an 8-bar phrase, create some kind of arrangement, and improvise a melody on top. There is nothing wrong with this approach at all. But I soon found myself learning towards the melody first. Not because I think it's better, but simply because it's the method I like right now.

Either way, it's a good idea to compose music using one approach or the other. If you try to harmonize a melody while you're creating it, it will slow you down and may stop the creative flow.

Composing For Piano - Don't Force, Allow

A student writes: "You always say, 'let the music tell you where it wants to go' but when I try to do this nothing comes. What to do?"

This is an excellent question because it really cuts to the core of my whole teaching philosophy which is -never force or try and "will" music into being. Instead, let it come of it's own accord.

To illustrate this, I'll share with you **my own process with "coming up" with material.**

Usually, I never have problems with the first 8-bars of music - sometimes called the (A) section. But once this section is down, so to speak, the rest of the music (if there is more to come) is usually more difficult for me.

I know from experience that if I try and force the music to move forward, I may get somewhere, but this music will usually sound stilted or lifeless. At this point I can do one of two things... I can walk away and hope for fresh inspiration at a later time or I can begin improvising without worrying or wondering about "more" music to come.

I know there is a school of thought that suggests you plunge forward and "make it happen." This can work and does work to get a product out there. The problem with this approach is what I mentioned previously. When your ego is involved in the creation process, your creation will be exactly that - ego centered.

When it comes from the source or spirit, you get a music that has that X factor. That indefinable quality that you can hear but quite can't put your finger on.

It really all comes down to process or product. Do you want a nice, neat product that can be admired by friends and family? Then it doesn't matter how you create music. But if you want a music that comes from a deeper place, don't force ... allow.

Composing
George Winston Style

I f you're a fan of New Age piano, no doubt you've listened to some of George Winston's music. What I find fascinating about his songs is how he creates them. Most improvisers/composers start with the melody, usually because it's the easiest way to begin.

What George does is start with the background. He creates an aural canvas over which he improvises the melody. This is an excellent way to create with because once you have the chord changes for the first 8-bars or so, you've pretty much finished a section of music.

Now after Winston gets his (A) section, it's another textural background that will usually make its appearance for the (B) section. The beautiful thing about this method is that it really frees up the right-hand! Once your left hand is playing the background, you are able to create melody easily. It's like a lead guitar player creating a solo while the band lays down the rhythm and chord changes. In fact, George Winston has referred to his left hand as the rhythm section.

Creating the background first is just another way to compose/improvise. There is absolutely nothing wrong with going with the melody first if that is what inspires you. However, it's good to know how others are creating so you can learn from them.

Composing Music - A New Approach

've always admired the method visual artists use to create with. They know what they're doing. And they understand how to go about finishing a painting. I wondered why music instruction couldn't be more like that.

Some of you may remember Bob Ross, the PBS painter with the big hair and serene smile. Now here was a guy who bypassed art school entirely - yet was able to create complete paintings in less than 30 minutes. Astonishing! And he could teach his method to others. I found this very inspiring.

My "method" is somewhat similar. Instead of giving you a palette of colors, I give you chords. Instead of creating a mountain landscape, you create aural landscapes. How? By understanding how to use your materials!

For example, in the lesson, "Reflections in Water," you use broken chord technique along with a few chords to improvise with. You see, once you have your materials and know how to use them, it makes creating very easy. You now can focus on capturing a mood and can actually play what you feel!

This is why artists ususally place the colors they'll be using for the painting they're working on out in the open. They make these decisions early on so the creative work is easier.

Composing Music - How To Compose A Theme and Variations for Piano

Recently, I posted a lesson where I show students how to compose a theme and variations for piano. Now, most composers today do not compose using this musical form. That's not to say it isn't still used but ... it can sound antiquated if certain harmonies and sounds are used.

For example, in the lesson, "August Reflections," I use the A harmonic minor scale and three chords from that scale to create a theme with three variations.

This particular sound has been used for quite a while. I chose it because it does sound familiar and some students wanted to learn something using a minor sounding scale.

Notice that the theme itself is quite simple. It consists of two 8-bar phrases that can be called A and B sections.

The two sections are played through and then the first variation begins. It consists of broken chords in the left hand. The second variation is a simple crossover pattern using the same chords -only this time, it's spread out. This gives the necessary contrast without breaking the "mood" of the piece.

The last variation is a play on the melody itself. I think I'm using eighth or sixteenth notes here as I just play around with breaking up the melody.

Finally, we return to the theme and there you have it... a complete piece of music using the theme and variations technique. A complete step by step breakdown of this lesson is available to course members.

To see this lesson for free on YouTube, go to:
http://youtube.com/watch?v=snyBgyBBNz4

Composing Using Chord Charts

A chord chart is a navigation tool. It's a way for the composer to chart out musical phrases and notate where chord changes occur.

It can be anywhere from 2-bars to 200 bars or more depending on how long the composition is or how many bars it takes to notate a musical idea.

For example, in the piece "Egrets," we have an 8-bar phrase with chord changes on top. This is a chord chart. It tells the performer where the chord changes occur, what the melody is, and when to change chords. This is all that is necessary to create a full arrangement of the music.

We don't need to write out every single note. We use the chord changes to create fresh arrangements of how we want the music to sound.

Notice that the first 2-bars of melody are written out. This was the initial idea. I then drew out 8-bars and finished by putting the chord changes on top. Now, whenever I want to play this little piece, I can play the initial melody and the whole thing comes together.

Of course, I could have written the whole thing out note for note, but this would have taken 30 times as long as just notating where the chords change.

Another benefit of this method is that the music is left elastic and fluid -that is, the aliveness of the music comes to you each and every time you play it. Why? Because each and every note is not written out. You can play it a little differently each time and each time the music will speak a little differently to you.

Composing Your Own Music - Easier Than You Think

Most teachers make composition so mysterious. First you have to learn harmony... then theory... then form and on and on it goes. But do you really have to learn all of this before launching your own creations? Absolutely not. and I'm living proof of that.

I don't have a degree in music yet I've managed to create and produce 2 solo piano CDs.

So, how did I do this? Well first, I had the desire. If you don't have this ingredient most anything you try and undertake will fail. Why? Because you need to have persistence. And persistence is something that works better when you want something badly. And I very badly wanted to create my own solo piano music.

Now, everyone has their own way and method of going about this. Mine was to first listen to pianists I love and admired - namely George Winston and John Herberman.

You see, besides persistence, you also need inspiration. And what better inspiration is there than to actually hear music you love and admire. In fact, I would listen to these CDs over and over. The music eventually seeped into me but this in and of itself is not enough.

Don't get me wrong ... there's nothing wrong with listening and saying to yourself "how did he do that?" In fact, I suggest students do exactly this. But you can jump over all this analyzing by learning just a little theory. And when I say little, I mean it.

What I have my students learn is something called the 8-bar phrase. And this is exactly what it sounds like. Once they get this -and it isn't hard to get -inroads into composition are quickly discovered.

For example, in the free workbook I offer with my course, you get tons of experience working with 8-bar phrases. You learn how to first improvise through them using chords. When you can do this - and it's pretty easy as well - you begin to "feel" how a composition is made up.

This approach has worked very well for me over the years as well as for my students.

Composing for Piano - Learn How to Improvise First!

When most people hear the word composer, they automatically think of classical composers like Mozart or Beethoven. This is the point where many "would be" composers freeze up because they tell themselves that their music could never be as good. And, this is also the point where would be music makers end their desire to create.

When you compare yourself to another person you are really defeating the whole idea of creating to begin with. Why? Because you're music is as unique as you are!

There will never be another person like you and there will never be anyone else who can create music like you. So give up your notions of becoming a great composer. Instead, focus on the joy that comes from being in the moment and creating your own music. To do this, learn how to improvise first.

You must have the ability to move forward without censoring what is coming out of you. Just like writers do with freewriting, so you too must do with improvisation.

Once you are able to just sit down at the piano and play without worrying if it's good enough, you'll be ready to put pen to paper and compose. Of course, you could compose without learning how to improvise, but chances are the music will sound stodgy and foursquare. It may not have the "life" that most composers shoot for.

Composing for Piano Using Small ABA Form

One of the most daunting tasks for beginners is composing music. Just the thought of it creates scary scenarios that demand perfection. But what if you actually knew what you were doing? Instead of fear, joy and a spirit of adventure would guide you to a finished piece of music. Let's look at how we might compose a small ABA form for piano.

The first thing I do is draw out 8-bars on a piece of paper. Any paper will do. You don't have to have ruled sheet music paper to compose...at least not the way I teach it. The reason I tell students to begin with 8-bars is that it's a very good space to work in. In fact, 8-bars is quite enough to give you your first (A) section. As an example, look at the lesson piece "A Peaceful Path."

Here, we have 3-4 minutes of music. We use the art of repetition and contrast and a small ABA form is generated.

If you listen to the piece, you'll hear where the (A) section ends and the (B) section begins. In fact, listening is very important. Most people listen to music as a complete aural experience and that's fine. But if you're interested in musical composition, you should also listen for the form of the piece. Most piano music is composed using sectional form.

For instance, here is the arrangement of the piece, "A Peaceful Path," - 2A2BA. This is a shorthand way of notating the amount of repeating that goes on in the piece. The first (A) section, 8-bars, is repeated twice, then the (B) section gets repeated twice and finally, we end up back where we started. The reason ABA form works so well is that it gives the listener a complete musical experience. And it gives them a sense of finality.

Sadly, the music must end somewhere and composers have been working on different ways to do this via the form of the piece. Many innovative composers have tried to abolish form but the question you must ask yourself is "Is this music giving the listener an emotional experience?" There's a good reason ABA form has been around for hundreds of years. Because it works!

Creating Stark Atmospheres

One of the things New Age pianist George Winston is known for is what he can do with just a few notes. In fact, in his piece Colors/Dance from the CD, "Autumn," he uses an ostinato pattern in his left hand to create a wonderful stark mood.

He creates this atmosphere by using a simple ostinato pattern in his left hand while the right improvises a melody. The trick to all of this is the way he lets the notes ring out. You really get to hear the overtones.

Also, he is a very percussive player, hitting the keys very hard. This contributes to the stark sound created. When I first heard this piece I was in awe! So captivating and alluring, the music instantly took me away and transported me into that wonderful nonverbal realm where magic happens.

Now, you too can create like this. In fact, it's quite easy once you get the ostinato pattern down in your left hand. Then, you can really have fun while you explore and create by improvising a melody with the right. Many New Age pianists employ the ostinato technique.

Creating Within Limits

When I first started playing the piano I wanted to learn how to compose. The idea that I could create something tangible really appealed to me.

So much so that I read everything I could get my hands on to learn the great art of musical composition. The problem was that these books assumed that you knew certain things like form, structure, harmony, and counterpoint. What a disappointment! It was hard trying to take the feelings I had on the inside and put them down on paper.

The real problem was that I had it backwards. Instead of trying to learn composition first, I needed to learn how to improvise - how to free the inner voice from criticism and judgement - so I could be free to create the music that was inside of me.

And so I began to read about how to improvise. Again, I was disappointed. I couldn't find good books on the subject, or books that would show me how to play in the New Age style - the style I loved. Eventually, I stumbled on a simple book that showed how to play using chord changes with 8-bar phrases. Now, here was something I could do! All I had to do now was learn chords. Once I knew how to play a few chords, I began to see that in order to really be creative there had to be a set of limitations. An irony, yet one that works!

By playing chord changes within a set framework, I was learning how to create within limits. Even so called "free improvisation" has certain rules. For example, you may decide that you'll improvise using the chords and scale of D Major. That's creating within limits. It's not necessary to use limits to create music, but it definitely helps one to focus in on expressing yourself. Instead of thinking about what to play, you've already made that decision and are now free to create.

Creating Your Own Compositions

The idea of actually creating a complete piece of music to play frightens many students. They just don't understand how someone could come up with something, put it down on paper, and call it their own.

The good news is that you don't need to read music to

compose. All you need is to understand a little about chords and musical phrases.

For example, in the lesson "Reflections in Water," we have 4 chords to create with. We have the order in which the chords are to be played -and then we play, creating an entire piece of music.

Now this piece is actually an improvisation. But if I wanted to "compose" this same piece, I would just draw bar lines, notate where the chords should be played, i.e. every 2-bars, every 4-bars, etc., and either pencil in the first 2-bars of melody, or record it so I could remember the melodic idea.

This is how I compose! I've been doing it for a very long time and it's a great method to quickly capture musical ideas. If I were to write out the same piece note for note, it would take hours! There's no need to do this because once you have your chord changes down and know the arrangement of the piece (Reflections in Water is a broken-chord arrangement) that's that!

Creating Your Own Unique Music

Have you ever dreamed of penning your own compositions? Writing music has been a dream of mine for the longest time. And it's a dream I am fortunate enough to have realized.

The idea of having a finished piece of music in front of you is exciting to say the least, but many students rush the process and end up with music that is less than what they originally thought of.

The way around this "composition trap," as I like to call it, is to be able to sit down at the piano or keyboard and be able to play for at least 15-20 minutes without judging what is coming out of you. Once you can do this, your ability to capture musical ideas as they first came to you increase.

First thoughts are powerful!

Your first ideas will ALWAYS BE YOUR BEST IDEAS! Why? Because this music comes straight from the heart and does not have the censorship of the critical mind attached to it. Always improvise first, then memorialize your ideas if you wish. I do this by jotting down an 8-bar section. Once the melody is recognized, I pencil in the first 2-bars and try to fill up the 8-bars with chord changes.

Once I have the first 8-bars, the whole piece is practically done. I usually do not finish a piece in one sitting, however, I do make it a point to at least get 8 bars of music down. This is a very doable goal and one you can accomplish as well!

Creative Dry Spells and What to Do About Them

A student recently emailed me saying that she was through with piano playing. She was very upset because the desire to play piano had disappeared. My sage advice? It happens to everyone!

Look, if we were meant to have the muse on 24/7 we would burn out faster than an accountant on espresso. There's something about the creative spark that does not like to be pressured. Sure, you can show up at the piano and try and enter in to the music, but if your spirit is not in it, chances are you're not going to want to play.

As frustrating as these "dry spells" can be, they are necessary for further creative growth. Patience is key here but many creative types (myself included) are not patient people. As I said before, forcing rarely works and will leave you even more frustrated. The only real solution to this is to see that we are more than who we are when we sit down to play the piano.

If we identify only with our creative self, we set ourselves up for frustration. It's also good to know that 99.9 times out of 100, creativity returns and we can relax and entertain the muse once more.

Don't Be Afraid of Melody

I n New Age piano music, there are basically two styles -textural and melodic. The textural style is usually associated with George Winston. You hear beautiful backgrounds created by the left hand while the right improvises melody.

The melodic style popularized by David Lanz places melody at the forefront.

Many students fall in love with the textural side of New Age piano. While there is nothing wrong at all with this, it's also a good idea to not put melody off to the side. It's a very good idea to familiarize yourself with both aspects of New Age piano playing.

For example, the piece "Egrets" focuses mostly on melody. In fact, the first thing you hear is the theme, which is, repeated two times more after the introduction. It's a simple theme that most would say is "New Age." In the lesson piece, "Cirrus," we have something entirely different! We have textures created by broken chords. Melody is not playing the lead role here. In fact, there really is no discernible melody at all - although there really is no music without melody - (a whole new topic!)

While I'm the first person to say, play what you feel and don't try and force yourself into playing something that's not your personal aesthetic, I'm also an advocate of not brushing off something completely just because it's not "your thing."

Leaning how to create pieces with melody at the forefront is a skill that will come in handy whether or not you enjoy this side of New Age piano.

Everything I Play Sounds the Same

Many students want to create music that has a certain emotional quality. For example, I once had a student ask me to show her how to play something that sounded happy.

Of course, this student missed the entire point of my teaching - to play emotionally and to not try and come up with something. I tried to explain to her that if she were feeling happy, then the natural outcome of the music would be flavored with this emotion.

As a natural outgrowth of the proceeding statement, there will be times, many times perhaps, when the music that comes out of you sounds the same. Many interpret this as being uncreative, when in fact, you are being true to yourself. When you don't try and come up with material, but instead, let the music come up, you are not forcing or willing the creative act. Instead, you are allowing yourself to express in the moment -whatever the sound may be.

If someone tells you that everything you play sounds the same, acknowledge it silently as a compliment and know that you are being true to yourself and the integrity of the artistic process!

When you are more concerned with enjoying the act of creating then trying to come up with material, you'll be way ahead of the game!

How I Compose a Piece of Music

A number of people have asked about my own methodology for creating a complete piece of music at the piano. At the risk of oversimplification, the steps are as follows:

1. I sit down at the piano without any thought of creating something and tune in to my feelings.

2. I start to play the first thing that comes to mind. In other words, my fingers come before my brain. I let it all hang out and see where the music wants to go. If something resonates or has energy I stay with it until

the energy dissipates. If the music does not seem to want to go anywhere I get up and leave.

3. Now, (assuming that I am on to something) I draw bar lines - enough for an 8-measure phrase. I then write down the chord changes on top - hopefully for the entire 8 bars. If the entire 8-bars don't come, I try for four - but I usually succeed in filling up this 8-bar space. I'll then pencil in the melody, but only the first 2-bars.

    This way, I let the rest of the melody come of its own accord. The first 2-bars is enough to allow me to improvise the rest until it gels into its final form.

4. After the first 8-bar section is complete (or incomplete, it doesn't matter), I'll write down another 8 or 4-bar phrase and listen for the next section of music - if there is a next section. If something comes, I follow the same procedure as above.

What I usually try for in this section is contrast. Something different. In this regard, I do usually start out with a preconceived idea of what the final form of the music will be. It will be A-B-A form 90% of the time. Knowing this allows me to use the techniques of composition (repetition and contrast) better.

Although this seems to contradict the idea of letting the music tell you where it wants to go (improvisation), it is useful in composition to give shape to the music. I explain this in more detail in my online class.

Now, I have the rudimentary parts of the entire piece. If I only have the A section and the B section does not want to come, I leave it and come back to it. Sometimes it never comes and that's all right too. I can then combine different sections to different pieces of music and all works out. I give it a title (nature titles for me, since that is my inspiration).

The piece is finished only after I play it a number of times and it has a chance to gel. I can't think of a better word for this process. After you play what you have written down a number of times, the music settles into what it will finally become. You just know when the piece is finished. It is an intuitive thing. Sometimes I'll repeat sections a number of times because the inspiration is fresh and because it feels right. Other pieces are very short because more repetition of a section just does not work.

How To Compose Your First Piano Piece

Many students love to improvise. But I'm often asked... "When can I learn how to actually create a complete piece of music?"

To which my response is "when do you want to begin?"

I often tell students that they should wait to learn how to compose until they can freely improvise on the piano. And when I say "freely" improvise, I mean being able to sit down and just play without criticizing what's coming out of you.

When you can do this, you'll be able to compose a piece of music without having to stop every 2-bars or so. Having said that - and assuming you're already able to freely improvise, let's see how to create our first real new age piano piece.

First, understand that most music is composed in sections. In fact, musical composition is just the art of repetition and contrast. The first thing I have students do is learn how to complete an 8-bar phrase. Once you can "fill up" this section with either melody or chords, your work is halfway done. Why? Because this 8-bar phrase can be used as your (A) section.

For example, take a look at the lesson "Ice Crystals." Here we have 8-bars for the (A) section and another 8-bars for the (B) section.

The chords are already indicated so all you have to do is improvise your way through. You see, once you can feel an 8-bar phrase, you'll be able to really "get" the idea of musical sections. And you'll be able to understand how composers use repetition and contrast to create an entire piece of music.

For "Ice Crystals," we have a small piece of music in ABA form. It lasts for a few minutes and then its over. The great thing about this lesson in particular is that you learn how to take an improvisation and use it to "fill up" the 8-bar phrases. A skill well worth learning!

How To Create An Original Melody From Scratch

There are 2 ways to create an original melody. The first has to do with improvisation. Here, you simply "come up" with material and either transfer it directly to sheet music or record it so it can be remembered later on.

The second way, and the one I'm going to show you how to do, is actually composing a melody from scratch. Some think this method (as opposed to free improvisation) is more difficult. Not if you use rhythmic patterns!

What are rhythmic patterns? They are simply note values, i.e. half notes, quarter notes, eight notes... etc.

Let me show you exactly what I mean...

Let's say you're walking around and a melody comes to you. Now most people do not have perfect pitch (myself included) and can't jot down the note qualities, i.e, a D note or an F sharp note. However, when you work with rhythmic patterns, you don't have to know the quality or name of the note, You just have to be able to jot down the pattern.

Here's how I do it. First, I only jot down the first 2-bars of the pattern. Why? Because this allows you to capture an idea without having to compose the whole thing on the spot. It's like a quick sketch visual artists might do. They capture the mood or feeling of a scene and later flesh out a full composition when they get home.

Now, you can draw out 2-bars anywhere. You don't need sheet music to do this and I never use sheet music. Any piece of paper will do. Then you simply notate the musical idea. For example, it might be something in 4/4 time. The first measure may be a half note and 2 quarter notes and the second measure could just be 4 quarter notes. With this idea, you can really remember your initial idea.

Remember Beethoven's Fifth Symphony? Of course, you don't remember the whole thing - but the first few notes you do... da da da duh... da da da duh...

This is the foundation for the entire symphony! That one rhythmic pattern. Of course, it took the musical genius of Beethoven to create an entire movement out of it but you get the idea.

In the lesson "Distant Shores," I show you how I do this step by step.

How To Create a Solo Piano CD - A Step by Step Approach!

S o, you want to know how someone creates an entire solo piano CD. It seems like a monumental task - and it is unless you break it down! Here's how I do it step by step.

Step One

The first thing I do is find the concept. I also consider this the most important aspect to creating an entire "album" of songs or pieces. Why? Because this is what gives you inspiration! For example, when I created my 2 CDs, "La Jolla Suite" and "Anza-Borrego Desert Suite," the first thing I did was find the concept or title I would be using for the CD - in this case, the two names you just read above.

You see, having this to start with gives you encouragement and inspiration to go on. This is because you can "see" the finished product. I remember quite well how excited I was when I first came up with the idea for "La Jolla Suite." La Jolla is a section of San Diego (a very beautiful section) that gave me all the artistic flow and energy I needed for completing it.

Step Two

Come up with your song titles. After the concept is identified and you know what you'll be working on, it's a good idea to flush out the entire album. Does this process remind you of anything? Yes, it's like what an author may do when preparing a book outline. Very similar indeed.

For La Jolla Suite, it was quite easy! I simply wrote out the places and things I loved the most about this fantastic place and the outline appeared very quickly. Another important aspect of the song identifying process is deciding on length. If your compositions tend towards the long side (7 minutes or more for each one), then plan on having 7 or 8 pieces. On the short side (3-5 minutes), plan on having many more. The goal is to create enough material for a 50-60 minute (or more) CD.

Step Three

Now, once you have the concept and the song titles, you're ready for the fun part. The song titles can actually suggest the mood of the piece! I remember when I was composing Sea Caves (a piece for La Jolla Suite). I kept repeating the words Sea Caves to myself then just went to the piano and literally "felt" the piece through. It came out to be a somewhat sad mood but that's exactly what I felt so it worked out.

This plan of action works well because you've already flushed out the outline for the entire CD. Now, the fun creative work can occupy your time. I think it took me a few months to completely finish all the pieces for La Jolla Suite. The rest of the time was spent in polishing them and getting them ready for performance.

So there you have it - a workable plan for creating an "album" or CD of your music!

How To Use Piano Chords To Create Complete Sections Of Music

Everyone wants to learn the "secret shortcuts" that will make improvising/composing music easier. And why not? Do you think professional composers don't use them? They do.

What I'm about to show you will have you blocking out sections of music in no time.

If you've been reading my articles about composition, you no doubt have heard me say that a **composition is the art of repetition and contrast**. And it's true! But before we get to the contrast part, we have to start somewhere. And that's where "sections" come in.

For example, in Lesson 4: "Morning Mist," we use a cross-over pattern in the left hand while the right hand improvises a melody. In fact, this is a perfect combination of improvisation and composition because what we have here is a 12 bar phrase repeated twice.

Now, in the lesson itself, I don't tell you it's a 12 bar phrase because I just wanted you to learn how to improvise. But, the fact is that's what this lesson is compositionally.

Here's what it looks like when charted out - chart for Morning Mist (pdf file)

Notice that only three chords are used here. But three chords are all we need to create this section of music. Essentially, this is a harmonic loop. We use the chords to create a background upon which we improvise our melodies.

Now, after improvising our melody, we may like what we hear and want to memorialize it thus turning this into a full-fledged composition.

The easiest way to create these harmonic loops is to simply pick a key, then a few chords from the key and start improvising with them. Then, when you feel like you're on to something you like, simply chart out when the chords change and that's that. You've created a harmonic loop.

How to Arrange Music for Piano

S o, how does one go about arranging piano music? That's a good question. And one that can get confusing for most students. They sometimes confuse composing with arranging and with good reason - they're closely connected. Let's look at how to arrange a piece of music for piano. Specifically, we'll look at the lesson piece "Fall Sunrise."

Fall Sunrise is a contemporary/new age piano piece I wrote to illustrate how ABA form works. The first section is comprised of 4-bars which is repeated twice. The next section (B) is an 8-bar phrase repeated twice and then we come back to our (A) section, which again is repeated twice. So, if we were to "arrange" this so we can see what it would look like we'd end up with something like this:

2A2B2A

This is a shorthand way of seeing the arrangement. It simply tells us how many times to repeat a section. Now, this arrangement by itself is sufficient for about 3-4 minutes of music, however, if we wanted to, we could add another section and lengthen it even more. The reason why we need another section (if we wanted more music) is that if we keep repeating this, it gets monotonous and boring.

We introduce a new section for contrast purposes. The ear hears this new music and is refreshed. But before we introduce a new section, we need something to lead us into it. We need what is called a transitionary phrase. Two bars is usually enough to accomplish this. The transition prepares the listener to receive something new. It's a connective device that bridges the sections. After the transition is introduced, we can bring in a new section of music and call it C.

Now, if we were to write out what this might look like we can come up with something like this:

2A2B2ATCA

Where T= transition and C= a new section of music. By adding in a new section, we can now repeat the other sections more because we've introduced contrast into the mix.

How to Capture a Mood Using a Few Chords

When a landscape artist wants to get the essence of a beautiful scene, they make a quick pencil sketch of it.

The artist doesn't want to represent the entire landscape as it is, but as they feel it to be. A few lines scribbled here and there indicate the feelings the artist wishes to convey. We musicians can do the same thing! We can quickly sketch out our ideas on paper by using chords and a chord chart.

A chord chart is just a way to notate when chords change through time. You can write out 8-bars to begin with (as I do). Now let us suppose you have the urge to capture something musically. What do you do? Well, for starters, you can pick a key to compose with.

For example, let's choose the Key of C. Now after deciding that, we know that the piece will have a Major sound to it. We also know that we have 6 chords to create with from the

C Major scale. With these primary decisions out of the way we now can focus on notating our musical ideas and capturing a mood. Here's how I do it:

I start by just improvising and letting the music come out naturally. For example, I play a C Maj. 7 chord and I like what I hear. I'll write down the first 2-bars of the melody, then place a chord symbol on top of the chart so I now have the musical idea in place.

My goal is to finish charting the 8-bar phrase with chords all the way through. Once this is accomplished I have the first section of music. If more is to come, I simply write out another 8-bar phrase and keep adding more music.

How to Compose Using ABA Form

ABA form is like a musical sandwich. You have the 2 slices of bread with the contrasting meat and cheese on the inside. Instead of bread and meat, you use musical materials. Perhaps an 8-bar phrase for the A section followed by a 4 or 8-bar phrase for the B section. A nice little musical sandwich.

A piece of music made from ABA form can last anywhere from 45 seconds to 5-6 minutes or longer **DEPENDING ON HOW THE COMPOSER UTILIZES THE TOOLS OF REPETITION AND CONTRAST!**

For example, I can take an 8-bar phrase, repeat that twice, play another 8 bars for the B section, then back to the A section again for another repeat (with variations of course). Now, how long will that last? It depends on tempo or how fast the piece moves through time. Most small ABA sections don't last longer than 2-3 minutes. Why? Because if they were repeated for longer periods of time, the music would become dull and repetitious.

BUT, if we create another section of music -the C section, it provides the relief the ear is searching for and we can then repeat the entire thing again so the form would look like this: ABACABA. This form extends ABA and provides the necessary contrast to create longer pieces.

How to Compose Your Own Music Using 8-bar Phrases

Some people think composing is this miraculous thing that only geniuses do. What a myth! It's a skill that can be learned. What can't be learned is the intuition that guides the creative force. What can be learned is the technique. And the most important part of composing technique has to do with THINKING IN PHRASES.

A musical phrase can be 2-bars long. It can be from 4 to 8-bars long as well. It is a unit of music that composers use, along with repetition and contrast to create ENTIRE SECTIONS OF MUSIC. There is no secret here, people. It's like building up a structure. That's why music is often referred to as frozen architecture. It is built up. The building up creates FORM. A structure such as ABA form can be composed of the A section (8-measures) B section (4 or more measures) then back to the A section.

Now you may be thinking, it looks logical but how does it transfer into actual music? Ah, this is where you get your feet wet and actually try composing a piece. We start from simple means and learn the principles of repetition and contrast first. We start with an 8-bar phrase for the A section.

Now a problem arises. How do I fill up this section? You can either start with the melody or with the chords. If you've had a chance to look at my free lesson, you'll see that by improvising, MATERIAL IS INSTANTLY CREATED! This solves your problem doesn't it? Now, you may be thinking, how do I get this material into the 8-bar framework you've been talking about? First, you need to be able to count in 3/4 or 4/4 time. Not very difficult but if you can't do this now, there are many sites on the web that can teach you this.

Now it's just a matter of transferring this raw improvisational material into the 8-bars. Most likely, you will be jotting down your chord changes. I explain this in a lot more detail in my online class. It's a quick sketch method. You have the raw uncensored germ coming from your improvisations -you then write down what chords you are playing and perhaps the first 2-bars of melody so you remember what the initial impulse was.

The reason I use the 8-bar phrase is that it is a nice unit of time to work with. I don't try and reinvent the wheel here. It's been used for centuries and can be used in New Age music as well. Once you have this 8-bar phrase you can repeat it and add in another section (B) to add contrast.

This may be hard to understand by just reading about it. You have to do it in order to really understand.

How to Create
Interesting Textures

A lot of new age piano music consists of repeating patterns, or textures in the left hand while the right hand improvises a melody. This approach is really a good one! It frees you up to create in the moment. First, you decide what chord or chords you'll be using in the left hand. You then create an ostinato or arpeggio that lays the foundation for the entire piece.

It's like the background a painter uses before the foreground is drawn in. In the case of music, the background would be the textural patterns in the left hand. Then the right hand comes in "to paint" in the rest of the picture - in this case, the improvised melody.

George Winston used this approach in the piece "Rain." First, you get this beautiful textural background created exclusively by the left hand. He covers more than an octave with the left hand using the thumb to reach past and make the music sound fuller. Now, in this piece he uses only a few chords, but interest is maintained through the improvised melody. In my piece, Flashflood, from Anza-Borrego Desert Suite, I use the same technique.

I start by playing an ostinato in the left, than add in the melody in the right. I keep playing the ostinato for as long as my intuition says, "this sounds good," then add in some contrast, either by changing chords, or by adding in new material.

It's important to realize that complete textural backgrounds can be created using the left hand alone. In fact, entire pieces of music can and have been created using this very versatile approach. It's especially suited for new age music. So, here's a step-by-step procedure for creating textures:

> Choose your chords -
>> These can be triads, or Open Position Chords, or any chord structure
>
> Create a pattern for your left hand
>
> Improvise a melody with your right hand

How to Create Your Own Beautiful Piano Compositions

You want to create your own music. Something you can put your name on and show off to friends and family. Why not? It's an amazing thing when you think about it. Where there was once nothing, now exists a piece of music authored by you. Let's examine how we might go about creating a complete piece of music.

Your initial idea is an important step. Why? Because the initial idea is the foundation for the entire piece! For example, let's say you get a certain melody in mind. You go to the piano and play it. But then you're stopped cold and don't know how or where to proceed next. What to do? You need to first draw out 8-bars on a piece of paper.

Working with an 8-bar phrase is the best way I know of capturing musical ideas and turning them into full-fledged compositions. You can write out as much of the melody as you can, or you can do what I do - write in the first 2-bars (the initial idea) and then use chords to quickly fill in the entire 8-bars. This example is if you work with melody first.

You can also "compose" working exclusively with chords. That is, you can take a few chords (like you have in the lesson, "Reflections in Water") and play around with them creating a few minutes of music. These chordal improvisations are a great way to get your ideas out. If you wanted to develop "Reflections in Water" or "compose" it, you'd have to put it on a chart and write out the chord symbols on top. Then, you'd have something you could go back to and play again if you wanted. You'd have a complete piece of music.

A long time ago, I read a book on musical composition where the author suggests you must work with either the melody or the chords and not both at once. This is an excellent suggestion because you simply cannot do both at once! It is far easier to either write out the melody for 8-bars or block out a chord arrangement than it is to do both at once.

How to Create Your Own Piano Compositions Quickly and Easily!

Here's one of my favorite methods for quickly blocking out entire sections of music and creating a complete piano composition.

First you need to draw out 8-bars on a piece of paper. I use 8-bars first because it's a relatively small space to "fill up" quickly. You don't have to use notation paper. Any paper will do. In fact, I use a spiral bound notebook with blank pages. I just write out 8-bars and voila, I've jotted down what will become a section of music.

Now, <u>here's the interesting part</u>. Most composers start with the melody line first. Nothing wrong with this, but if you really want to zap out a section quickly, start with the chord changes. Why? Because you can block out bars of music faster. Here's what I mean.

Say you want to create something in the Key of F Major. Great. Now we know that we have at least six chords to work with. By using just three chords, we can block out our 8-bars. How? Look... Say we have the F Major 7 chord for the first 4 bars, then comes B flat Major for 2-bars and C 7 for the last 2-bars. We have now created a chord progression and charted it out. You can do this in under a minute. I swear it! It's that easy. Now all you have to do is decide upon the kind of arrangement you'll create for these chords.

It might be arpeggios, block chords, open position chords... whatever. The point here is that by using chords, you can map out a harmonic territory. Now you can either create a melody using these chords, or keep it entirely textural. It's up to you! Try it.

How to Create a Theme and Variations for Piano!

There are many ways to compose a piece of music. ABA forms, sonata allegro form, and so on. But the humble theme and variations has been around for centuries. While not used nearly as much as it was during the classical period, it still can be used to create artistic and attractive contemporary piano pieces. Let's get started!

First, we need a theme! Eight bars are the perfect size to contain your theme. I work within this framework all the time and it has proven to be a workhorse when it comes to capturing musical ideas. Now, we can either begin with chords or melody. For theme and variations, I like to start with the melody (as do most composers.) This is because it's a lot easier to create variations for a simple melody than it is to create different textures for chord changes.

The melody does not (and should not) be sophisticated for theme and variations. Why? Because we want to change the melody. It's a lot easier to vary a simple theme than it is a complex one, although I'm sure it's been done successfully. Look at "Pachelbel's Canon in D" as an example. The theme is simple yet beautiful - exactly what we want.

Once the first 8-bars is complete, we harmonize it and we have the complete theme. Now we create variation one. Most theme and variations composed by the "masters" start their initial variations with just a little change and gradually vary the theme to where it may be unrecognizable towards the end.

We don't have to do this here. In fact, I suggest beginners only create 3 variations at the most. Look at it as an arc. You start out with something, let's say something andante, or slow. Now we want to add some contrast to the whole thing so around variations 2 or 3 we speed it up a little. Eventually we close the theme and variations by returning to the original theme. Take a look at the author's lesson #54 for a good example of how to do this.

How to Create
an Original Melody

Here's a method I use that works. First, sit down at your piano or keyboard and just improvise. I suggest improvising first because music that is created in this way is at its freshest. It's not adulterated or thought up. It is pure inspiration. Now, there will come times during improvisation where you may say to yourself, "this is nice and I'd like to develop it." You see, now you have an original melody to develop.

The trick is you don't need a lot of material to begin with. JUST TWO BARS IS ENOUGH to start you on your way. I usually work within 8-bar phrases so I know that the melody will usually end or repeat itself after 8-bars. I say usually because sometimes, the melody does not want to fit nice and neat into a predefined 8-bar phrase. But more times than not, the 8-bar phrase will serve you well

Now, to be able to grow the initial 2-bars of inspired melody into 8, you can either harmonize the melody with a few chords or just write out the rest of the melody as it comes. Once I have the first 2-bars, I usually have already identified what Key the piece will be in. It then becomes a matter of choosing a few chords from the Key and the rest of the material is easily flushed out into 8-bars. In the piece "Rainforest," I use 2 chords for an entire 8-bar phrase (4-bars for G Maj. and 4 for E-minor) and improvise the melody on top.

How to Find Musical Ideas

The Russian Composer Igor Stravinsky once said: " A good composer does not imitate; he steals."

I think what he meant by this is that it's OK to use a technique developed by another and make it your own. To imitate is to steal a technique or style and, somehow, not incorporate your own voice and energy into it.

We all get our ideas from somewhere, whether by accidentally listening to a piece of music and subconsciously storing it away, or by a conscious act where we say to ourselves: "This sounds great and I want to use it in my own music."

Some people have the idea that everything created must be original with no outside influences -but this is unrealistic. Haydn taught Beethoven. Italian composers influenced Bach and so on. All past and present composers on this planet have their influences whether they admit them or not.

Now, most of you know that I have two major influences: George Winston and John Herberman. You may or may not know of these people. The point is I admit that they shaped my own style. How? Because I liked listening to them. It's that simple.

When I sit down to play, I inevitably gravitate towards one style or the other. I'm fine with that. It doesn't mean that I'm unoriginal. It just means that I acknowledge reality and don't try to come up with "something original." What sounds new is 99.9 times out of 100, a modification of what came before.

The whole point I'm trying to make is this: Don't try to be original. Instead, focus on what you like and love and your own voice will come through in the end. The music may be modified to an extreme (innovation) or just a little (homage). Just don't imitate.

How to Get Past Creative Blocks

When I first began playing the piano and improvising, there were times when the music just wouldn't flow. No matter what I did, I couldn't make it go any further. Blocked and frustrated, I wondered why this happened. One minute, I would be in flow and enjoying the process of playing the piano. The next, I would find myself trying to come up with material.

I soon realized that the more I tried to "come up" with something, the more blocked I became. The solution to this particular problem is simple, yet many find it to be frustrating in itself.

The answer is simply to walk away. That's right! If you're playing the piano and it just won't come anymore, I suggest getting up and finding something else to do. Why? Because you can not force play! It's that simple. And that difficult because we want to get back into the "groove." But getting back to this place requires you to ease up a bit.

You see, the creative process is somewhat similar to meditation. Meditation can't be forced or willed into working. It must be allowed to work. So too, the creative process. There are times when I won't touch the piano for weeks on end. This used to bother me until I saw that I needed time away - a regenerative period so to speak.

Natalie Goldberg of "*Writing Down the Bones*" fame describes this lackluster period as composting. Don't worry about losing your creative ability. You never lost it. Just give it time to compost and when you return to the music, you will hear something new and wonderful!

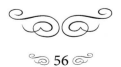

How to Quickly and Easily Block out Entire Sections of Music

Most of you don't want to go to college and learn theory, harmony, and composition techniques. Not only is it tedious and for the most part boring, but it's also unnecessary.

That is, if you want to compose atonal music or whatever the latest fad in academia is, go to college. If you want to capture your ideas and quickly put them down on paper, you only need to learn how to think in phrases!

This is what most improvisers/composers do anyway. For example, many of you have heard me speak of using 8-bar phrases as a cornerstone to both improv and composition. Why? Because it's a very easy space to work in! You can very quickly complete 8-bars and have both your theme and the first section of music.

By working this way, you don't have to worry about what the final form of the piece will be. Many composition books suggest you block out the entire structure of the piece first including harmony, climax, etc. This is one way of working with music. It's not the only way.

Especially for beginners, it can be daunting to say the least to have no idea where you're going and what to do next. But, and here's the really good part, by working with 8-bar phrases, you learn how smaller sections are built into larger sections and so on. In other words, you learn how composers think.

Here's how I do it. I start by improvising and see what comes up. If I feel like I'm on to something, I just write out 8-bars on a sheet of paper (any paper will do) notate what key I'm playing in and the time and write out the first 2-bars of the melodic idea. Next, I'll play through and write out the chord changes. For example, if the piece is in the key of F Major, the first 2-bars may be an F Major chord, the next 2-bars, B flat Major and so on.

By working this way, you can quickly complete an 8-bar section of music and you're ready to add more sections working the same way!

How to Use Chord Changes to Learn the Art of Musical Composition

When I first started getting interested in composing it dumbfounded me. So many questions. The number one question I had was how did they do it? How do you create something and build a complete piece of music?

Intrigued, I searched every book on the subject of music composition I could find. Living in San Diego as I do, the libraries aren't the best. I found books on harmony, theory, and composition. But they all were over my head AND they all gave examples that seemed antiquated and dull. Eventually though, if you persist, you'll always find at least one or two books that will be helpful and I did. I found this one book that had chord changes mapped out in 8-bar sections. Now here was something I could understand!

No note reading was required here. All I needed to do was play a few chords on the piano and be able to keep time -both of which I could do. After playing the chord changes for a while, I started to feel what musical form was. It no longer was an academic exercise. Not at all. You see, when I played through the chord changes in 4/4 time, I actually felt the form! That is, after the 8-bars was played, I knew that I could either repeat them again, or play new material (another new 8-bar phrase.) And that's all there is really to musical composition. Composition is the art of repetition and contrast.

Now, just saying this won't teach you anything. That's why when I read this in a book, I understood it, but didn't really know how to do it. By following simple chord changes, the body actually takes in the rhythm and you start to feel what an 8-bar phrase is. By doing this, you intuitively begin to understand what form is all about.

For instance, in the lesson piece "Fall Sunrise," we have something called an ABA form. We have 4-bars repeated twice for the first section (A), then an 8-bar phrase repeated twice for the (B) section. When we use the art of repetition and contrast, we get the common ABA form used so much in musical composition.

Musical Composition - How To Listen To Music Like A Composer

D id you know that there is more than one way to listen to music? I first read about this from a small book by composer Aaron Copeland.

You see most people listen to music as if something were

washing over them. They listen to the oncoming barrage of notes and chords and never wonder or understand how it achieves the effect it does.

Not composers. They listen differently. While most people enjoy music for music's sake -a composer listens for sections or how the music is constructed.

I'm not saying that composers never listen to music for pure enjoyment. That would be terrible. No. What I'm saying is that a composer or anyone who takes the time to learn, can begin to hear how music is put together.

Most music created today is comprised of sections. More specifically, we have A and B sections, introductions, transitions and endings and so on.

All these "pieces" go into creating a piece of music. Even spontaneously improvised pieces of music have been given a name by composers. They call it "through composed" which means that there are no distinctly repeating sections.

For example, take the lesson "Cirrus." (You can listen to this lesson at quiescencemusic.com) It starts out with a few notes that, by themselves, seem to go nowhere. But, if you listen to the entire piece of music, you'll begin to hear sections. Musical composition is the art of repetition and contrast. This is what composers listen for. They listen to see how the songwriter uses these two qualities. The piece "Cirrus" was actually an improvised piece but it turns out that even with this, you can hear that repetition and contrast was used.

This can be done consciously, as many composers do as they create a piece, or simply generated spontaneously as in the case of "Cirrus."

New Age Pianist Shows You How To Compose Your Own Music

This New Age pianist has been playing piano for over 15 years now, and while I'm constantly learning new things, the one thing that's helped me out -as far as composing goes - is **looking at music as sections.**

I'm always telling my students to work within an 8-bar framework. Why 8-bars? Because it's a nice, neat time space to work in. And, more importantly, it doesn't overwhelm beginning students who feel they must come up with 100 bars at their first attempt.

The beauty of working within this framework is that it teaches you about phrases. Music has been compared to writing in the sense that it's made up of small phrases (like sentences) bigger sections.. periods of music (like paragraphs) and finally, complete movements (chapters).

Composers always think in sections because they know this is how music is constructed, in at least 99% of the music in the western world.

When you master the 8-bar phrase, you learn how to complete a section of music. You learn that the art of composition has everything to do with repetition and contrast.

There's only so many times you can repeat an 8-bar phrase before it gets stagnant. Here is where we introduce new material - a contrasting section. Perhaps another 8-bars or so.

Another thing I have my students do is learn how to create a complete ABA form.

This musical form is the most common one used and it's also quite easy to create. Once the first 8-bar phrase is complete (the A section) it's time for some contrast. Maybe 4-bars... perhaps eight or more will do the trick here. Finally, the first A section is repeated (with some variation) and that's that - a small ABA form is finished.

It's a good idea to master these small sections of music before delving into 400 bar compositions.

New Age Piano Tricks

One of the things that makes New Age piano so enjoyable is that it's easy to get started.

One of the "tricks" of the trade is to play an ostinato pattern in the left-hand while the right improvises a melody. Just listen to George Winston's lovely piece, "Colors/Dance," to hear an excellent example of this technique.

He uses just two chords in the beginning. But just look what he does with them! He maintains interest for a good couple of minutes before any contrast is introduced. Remarkable! And not as easy to do as many people think!

The artistry in this is how he maintains interest. The improvised right-hand melody carries the music through and propels listener attention forward. The left-hand, however, is just playing the same ostinato pattern.

Complicated? Hardly. A beautiful piece of music? Absolutely. And all that's required is the ability to trust your intuition. Trusting intuition is THE MOST IMPORTANT THING A TEACHER CAN HELP YOU LEARN! Why? Because when you trust yourself, you allow the music to come as it should - naturally and easily.

Technique can be taught by most anyone and can be learned readily. However, the ability to trust yourself is something that takes a bit of introspection. Most of us have an internal critic that tries to condemn any creative effort. We must learn to listen to what we say to ourselves and allow for the creative impulse.

Paint Your Own Musical Landscapes!

I don't know why, but I find the idea of interpreting nature musically to be very appealing. Maybe it's because I'm attracted to nature's beauty, but the notion of communicating that beauty musically has always intrigued me.

Not being a very patient person, I wanted to find a way to capture a musical idea very quickly and sketch out an entire piece all at once. Visual artists do something called a thumbnail sketch and I wanted to do the same thing for music.

It then occurred to me that if I just sketch out the first 8-bars of the piece, and write in the first 2-bars of melody, I could capture an idea that would be remembered weeks or even years later. It's amazing but this actually works! The secret is the melody.

If you can't read music and want to do this just do what I do. I write down the note values (quarter notes, half notes., etc.) and write the letter name of the note beside the note value. One of the most important things I've discovered over the years is that the note value (its time length) is what really captures the idea. Just think of Beethoven's Fifth Symphony for a good example. Da Da Da Duh... These notes mark the whole composition.

Piano Composition Secret of George Winston Reveals Easy Way to Play Piano!

Love him or hate him, George Winston single handedly invented a whole new genre of music - New Age piano. His light, ambient sound has reached millions of listeners around the world.

Now, a lot, and I mean a lot of pianists would like to be able to play like George but don't think they can. That is, they don't know how he does what he does. They think he just sits down and music comes up or, they believe that he spent years studying composition and theory in order to create these sometimes elaborate compositions.

But, and here's the interesting thing, when you really listen and break down what he's doing (and most other composers for that matter) it's all about how phrases of music are repeated and then contrasted with new material. That's it! That's all composition is. It's the art of repetition and contrast!

Just saying this won't help you understand how it's done though. For example, in the author's lesson, "Winter Scene," we have a repeating ostinato pattern using two chords. The pattern is played over and over again while the right hand improvises a melody. And guess what? That's a piece of music! That's right! Now, if I wanted to show this piece as a composition, I would have to chart it out using a chord chart. This too is a lot easier than it sounds.

For instance, "Winter Scene" is just a 4-bar phrase in 4/4 time. Each chord gets 2 bars and that's it! Sometimes called a "loop" these phrases can be repeated as long as the composer/improviser wishes. Then, if more music is required, we just add in new phrases and keep building up our piece of music.

So what is George Winston's secret? Learn how to use musical phrases to create your own easy compositions!

Piano Journeys - Create Your Own Unique Music!

Have you ever marveled at how artists can quickly sketch out a beautiful landscape scene and convert it into a full-fledged painting? I have and I've always been jealous of their ability to do so.

I've often wondered why music couldn't be more like this. Of course, composers know how to create a complete piece of music, but I didn't want to spend years learning theory and harmonic analysis. I didn't want to study form and compositional technique. Not because I was lazy or unmotivated, but because there had to be a simpler way of taking what I felt inside and turning it into a piano improvisation or composition.

Fortunately for me, I discovered my own unique method for quickly creating what I love to create and that is New Age piano music.

A few chords and a key in which to play are all I needed to begin quickly creating my own unique piano journeys. You see, the problem most aspiring composers have is that they think they need to learn everything that was ever written about how to compose music. This isn't necessary and only serves to delay the experience of jumping in the water and trying it first hand.

My method is really simple - improvise first and let the music tell you where it wants to go. That is, let go and allow the music to flow through you. I ALWAYS START WITH IMPROVISATION because this is where the raw creative energy is. If something strikes me as particularly nice, I'll draw out 8-bars on a sheet of paper. It doesn't have to be notation paper either. I just use a blank composition journal I bought at a bookstore to do this.

After the 8-bars is drawn, I'll write in the first 2-bars of the melody to remember the initial idea. I then use the chords from the key I'm working in to complete this small 8-bar section. Working within 8-bar sections is, I think, the best way a beginner can actually complete a musical phrase. It's a very attainable goal and works very well.

Piano Lessons: Creating an Impressionistic Soundscape

Ah... the Soundscape. That indefinable rush of notes that envelopes and soothes. The first classical composer to really embrace this type of music was Claude Debussy.

In fact, a whole style of music, Impressionism, was coined based on his music alone.

It's a lush style that tries to steer clear of too definable a melody line. Instead, textures and rhythms are explored.

Some students think this style is the hardest to learn, but I think it's actually easier to play this style than the straight melodic style embraced in the classical period.

For the improvising pianist, creating an impressionist Soundscape requires nothing more than learning a few chords and playing them.

Debussy based much of his music on something called the whole-tone scale. This scale basically takes out any "tension" that can be found in our major and minor scales. The Chinese and Japanese use pentatonic scales frequently and this is also similar.

But, we don't have to use these scales to create our Soundscape. The C Major scale will work just fine. For instance, in the lesson **"Reflections in Water,"** we use open position chords to create with. It's HOW we use them that gives us the feeling of a Soundscape.

We play slowly and allow the notes to ring out. No rushing is involved here. Instead, we adapt an attitude of exploration. The music is created by allowing our fingers to play with the tones in the C Major scale. Chord changes come every few bars or so. The music is repeated a few times and then we stop.

You see, you don't need fancy materials to create beautiful Soundscapes with. You can use just a few chords from the C Major scale and improvise a beautiful piece of music! We play with the textures and allow the music to appear - without forcing or willing it into being.

Piano Songs - Create Them Yourself With Just a Few Chords!

Most people play other people's music. That's fine. Nothing wrong with that. The classical repertoire is fantastic and worthy of playing.

But what if you want to just sit down at the piano and create on your own? Piano songs can come out of you as easily as drinking a glass of water. Think not? It's true. All you need to realize is it can be done -if you start using a chord-based approach!

For example, in the lesson "Reflections in Water" (available at quiescencemusic.com), a few chords and a simple technique is used to create a very nice little piano song.

Nothing complicated or sophisticated here. Just some simple chords in open position and a framework upon which to hang it.

But, and this is important, it's an original piece of music. No note-reading was used. No attempt to "come up" with material. You see, when you're able to freely improvise, piano songs can spill out of you as easy as words do when speaking.

So what's the trick? It's being able to let go of the need to control the outcome and allow the music to unfold on it's own. This is actually an intuitive approach to playing the piano and one that's served me well over the past 15 years.

Look, the goal for most piano players is to be able to either play the classics, or play from lead sheets or fake books. Creating one's own piano music is a foreign notion to most. **That's why I'm a big fan of the New Age piano style!**

It focuses mainly on improvisation and "free play" and requires very little in the way of technical know how. What is required is the ability to suspend judgment and allow for the unexpected.

This can be very threatening to some. In fact, people come up with all kinds of excuses as to why this music is "inferior" to other types. I always laugh when I hear that argument because I know there's nothing more these people want then just to "be" at the piano.

Piano Songs - Create Them Yourself!

Have you ever wanted to create your own unique piano songs? Just simple pieces that express how you feel? You can if you learn how to improvise first and then learn how to compose. Here's why.

Improvising allows you to express what you feel without constraint. In essence, it's like free writing because the goal here is to free your own unique voice without having to worry about right or wrong, good or bad. It is a skill that students should learn before any other and is foundational for further success at composing. Once you are able to sit down at the piano and can trust your intuition to guide you, you're ready to compose.

Composition is really just slowed down improvisation. We take the initial inspirational gem we've discovered through improv and flush it out using the tools of repetition and contrast. For example, in the lesson "Waiting for Spring," we learn how to create a simple ABA form in the Key of C.

The key here is that we already know the piece will be an ABA form so how do we proceed? Easily! The way I do it is I write out the first 8-bars and then improvise to see what will come up. Once I'm onto something, I write out the first 2-bars of the melody so I can remember it. Then I use chords from the Key of C Major to finish the first 8-bars; my (A) section. Another 8-bars or so for my (B) section and I'm done! The arrangement of this easy piano song usually works itself out to be play the (A) section twice, (B) section once, back to the (A) section and I'm done. Most of the time, this comes out to about 2-3 minutes of music.

The important thing for creating your own piano songs is that you must be able to move forward and complete sections of music. This is best accomplished when you can improvise freely first!

Play and Compose New Age Piano Now - Even if You've Never Touched a Keyboard!

You love the sound of New Age piano. You may have wondered how certain people can just sit down at the piano and start playing from scratch. It's not magic! It's called knowing what you're doing and you can do the same! To begin, you need to know a few chords. I suggest complete beginners start out with something called the open position chord. This chord structure has many, many benefits for the beginner (and advanced student!)

First, it's a modern sounding chord. Forget about triads and scales. The open position chord allows you to play seventh chords right away. This chord structure is used by most jazz and contemporary piano players.

Second, <u>it uses both hands right away!</u> When you first finger this chord structure, it will stretch your hands out completely. In fact, you will be playing more than 2 octaves of the piano keyboard. This is something beginners want to do right away and it can be done with a minimum of practice.

Let's look at how we can use this chord structure to create music with. In the lesson, "Reflections in Water," we have 4 chords to play. The chords are in the Key of C major, which means they are all located on the white keys. We finger the first chord (C Major 7) with both hands and notice the sound. How open it is! The sound you get from this chord is perfect for the New Age sound. In fact, once we finger this chord, we only have to move our fingers around a little and music comes out. It's really an amazing thing.

We switch chords using the same fingering and play around with the notes from the C major scale. This is all that is required to create New Age piano music or Jazz music for that matter. The amazing thing about this chord type is the amount of music you can create right from the start. If you're into New Age piano and want to immediately play in this style, I highly recommend you learn how to play the open position piano chord!

Relaxing Piano Music - Create It Yourself With These Easy to Follow Piano Lessons

You love the soothing sounds of relaxing piano music. But have you ever thought about actually going to your piano and creating it yourself?

Edward Weiss's online piano course teaches beginning adult students how to play piano using a chord-based approach. The lessons are designed in an easy step by step fashion that shows you what chords to play and how to improvise and create your own music.

You already know how therapeutic listening to solo piano music is. Creating it on your own is much better because you're actually involved in the process. Making music forces you to be in the present. Once you get a taste of how good this feels, you'll want more and more.

For instance, take the free lesson "Winter Scene." Here we have a relaxing piano lesson that teaches you to play 2 chords in your left hand while your right improvises melody.

To the complete beginner, this may seem like a lot. And it is until you actually try it. Once you start to play the chords in your left hand and get the pattern down, it becomes quite simple to jump in with the right and begin improvising a melody.

I always advise students to go as slow as they need to at first. Speed is not important at all. Playing with sensitivity is. If all you can do is play one note in the right hand while your left is busy playing, than you've accomplished quite a lot.

It won't take long for you to freely improvise and create your own relaxing piano music!

Simple ABA Form - Creating Your Own Piano Compositions!

Form... to give shape to something. Yes, form is about giving music shape. Odd as this sounds (because we can't see music), there can be a definable shape to our creations. One of the more frequently used forms is called ABA.

This means we play a section of music 1 or 2 times, we play another (B) and then we return to our first section. Seems simple enough right? Yet many students have trouble creating their own piano compositions using this simple form. Most likely, this has to do with thinking too much.

Many students over think things and make their job of music creation that much harder. It doesn't have to be that way. Not if you think in phrases! For example, take the lesson, "Rainforest Revisited."

Here we return to Lesson 3: "Rainforest" which is basically an extended improvisation. In "Rainforest Revisited," you're shown how to add another section of music - a contrasting (B) section to create a new piece of music in ABA form.

Now, most of you have no trouble when it comes to improvising and just playing the piano. Your music flows out of you and this is how it should be. The problem comes when students try and think about what comes next. Wrong approach! Don't think! Continue your next section the same way - by using your intuition.

Here's how I came up with the (B) section for "Rainforest Revisited." I simply sat down at the piano, played the original "Rainforest" piece and allowed my intuition to guide me to the next section. I didn't ask "what should come next?" No. I felt my way through. I knew the (B) section would be 8-bars or so long and just came up with something contrasting to the original "Rainforest." I now had a (B) section and could turn the entire thing into an ABA form piece of music!

The Secret to Composition

When I first started out playing piano and trying to compose, I couldn't figure out how someone could get his or her inspiration down on paper.

It was very frustrating to look at and listen to other artists who seemed to know the "secret" to composition.

Little did I know that the big secret really isn't about composing - it's about being able to trust your own intuition and let it lead you instead of the other way around. It took a long while before I was able to just let go and allow the music to flow out. But once I could do this, the idea of capturing an idea didn't seem to matter so much. No. It was more important for me to let it all go.

It also occurred to me that the more I tried to "capture" an idea, the harder it was to get down. Another artistic irony that's proved itself over the years.

Many people who want to compose their own music have problems because they believe that the musical idea they are working on is holy. They don't understand that there are literally millions of ideas waiting to be born. If they loosened their grip slightly, they would be able to gently notate that idea and see where it would lead them. An entirely different approach and one that allows for so called errors, mistakes, etc.

For me, the secret to composing is not knowing how to capture a musical idea. It's being able to open up to the limitless ideas within and allowing them to express naturally through improvisation.

To Learn How to Compose, Learn How to Improvise

As I sit here writing this, listening to Mozart, I can't help but think of musical form. That sometimes, but often not, discernible quality to music that makes it art. And when I say art, I'm not talking about improvisation or free form. I'm talking about composition.

Most students are baffled as to how a piece of music is constructed. It's as if learning how to compose is something only gifted individuals do. And while the intuitive sense behind creating melody itself can not be taught, the craft can!

Form is to music what flower arranging is to the florist. You see, it's all about creating a structure. In flower arranging, the goal is to create something pleasing to the eye. This is accomplished by how the florist places the flowers. He's not going to stack them all to one side. No. He wants to create something that allows the eye to go back and forth. Something that the viewer can take as a complete experience. Music is much the same way.

If we played the same thing over and over, we get monotony. If we vary the music too much, we get incoherence. The solution? Go back and forth between sections! Now, this is easy to grasp intellectually. The difficulty comes when students attempt to create their first composition and end up with something less than satisfactory. And this is because most students haven't learned to trust their intuition.

You see, to be able to compose, you must have the ability to move forward without criticizing yourself. This is THE most important skill and one that can be developed through learning how to improvise. I always suggest students learn how to improvise first. Then, when the internal critic is gone, they can move forward with their ideas. It seems strange that improvisation should come before composition but if you want to develop quickly you do really need to free yourself from judging the product and have the ability to move forward. Then, when you learn how to compose by using sections, you won't be as daunted and stuck at every little detail.

You Can Compose Your Own Music!

Whenever someone uses the word composer, inevitably, the names of Beethoven, Bach, and other classical personages come to mind. This can be very intimidating to those who want to record their musical thoughts and ideas down.

In fact, comparing yourself to ANY composer will be detrimental to you. Why? Because you will always have to live up to someone's expectations of what is good music or what is not good music. This comparison trap will lead you nowhere and will result in a drying up of the creative spirit. The solution to this trap is to begin where you are and for most of us that means begin EASY!

I'll never forget the first time I tried to "compose" something. It was for classical guitar. I tried to create something original and it took me 2 hours just to write out 4-bars of melody. Of course, I didn't know what I was doing. There has to be some kind of method that works for you. Now, the method I use today has been very easy to work with because it gives me the freedom to compose AND improvise at the same time. I "compose" using 8-bar phrases.

To do this all one has to do is write out 8-bars on a sheet of paper. Any paper will do. It doesn't have to be music paper or manuscript. In fact, I just use a spiral bound journal with ruled lines on it. Whenever I want to memorialize an idea, I draw out 8-bars very quickly. I then improvise and allow myself the freedom to play anything that comes out of me. If I try and think something up, the music will usually wind up sounding forced or contrived - qualities that music is better off not having.

Once the idea (either melodic or textural) appears, I write out the first 2-bars so I remember what it is and use chords to quickly fill in the 8-bar section. After this is completed, I may draw another 8-bars and see what else comes. If nothing more is coming at this particular point, I put the journal away and come back to it later on. This method has served me well over the years and is an excellent starting method for beginning composers.

Improvisation

Avoid These 3 Common Mistakes When Improvising

Mistake #1 - Thinking about what you're going to play

A lot of students think there should be some kind of preparation before improvising on the piano. They are right! There should be some thought as to the sound, tonality, and key but once these choices are made the thinking should stop and the playing should begin.

Mistake #2 - Worrying about whether it's good or not

Are you concerned with how your music sounds? Many students are. This mistake is prevalent among newbies at improvisation. They play a key or two and then think it stinks. Nothing will stop the creative flow more than thinking that what's coming out of you is not good enough! Good is in the ear of the beholder. That beholder is you so stop judging the product and focus on enjoying the process of being in the moment. This is why people learn to improvise in the first place. Let go and let the music tell you where it wants to go!

Mistake #3 - Thinking that you don't know enough to improvise

This mistake is really an oxymoron because the more you

know, the more likely it is that you will experience blocks. If you do not have a lot of formal music knowledge, don't let that stop you. All you need to know in order to improvise is chords and the scale the chords came from. That's it. And the good news is this is easily learned.

Some students create unnecessary problems for themselves because they believe they need to know this or that before they can begin. This is just an excuse to avoid jumping in the water. It's also a way to avoid the act itself because once you begin to play you may tell yourself you really don't know what you're doing. Trust me. You know enough and you know enough to begin now.

Create A Fantastic Sounding Piano Improvisation Using Just One Chord!

You'd be amazed to find out that some of the most complex sounding pieces of music are actually simple to create. Take the piano lesson, "Caverns," for example. Here we use just one chord in the left hand to create a harmonic foundation for the right hand improvisation.

The right hand plays both melody and bass notes but the left is just playing one chord. The sound that is created is full and rich! But how can this be? After all, only one chord is used. The secret is in how the chord is played.

We use a simple ostinato pattern to create the backdrop.

This backdrop is the key to the whole piece. It quietly goes on in the background while the right hand is busy playing melody. Bass notes are also called into play with the right hand crossing over the left. Back and forth the right hand goes and we end up with 2 minutes of music using just one chord!

This is an excellent example of the power of limits. We know what the chord will be - in this case D minor. We know that we will be playing melody notes from the D Dorian mode. Now we can relax and enjoy the act of making music. With the decisions of what to play out of the way, it makes the act of creating all that easier.

Creating A Piano Improvisation - The Making of December Twilight

"How is it done?" asked one student. "How do you create something like December Twilight?" I'll tell you but you may be surprised at the answer.

December Twilight is a lesson piece (available at quiescence-music.com) I created to teach students hand independence. So, how did I create it? I haven't the slightest idea.

What I mean is, I went over to the piano like I usually do, sat down, and just started to play around. And out of nowhere, I found myself reaching for a bass note followed by an A major triad and D major chord.

Now, I'm not saying this to mystify you, but when you operate this way on the piano, the unexpected comes up. I wasn't "trying" for anything here. I allowed myself to just be at the keyboard and with this attitude, the music that comes is always a surprise and here's the best part - **this approach always leads to the freshest sounding music!**

Once the initial idea came - a left-hand ostinato pattern using a good portion of the keyboard, the rest was easy enough and that had to do with simply improvising a melody in the right hand.

Many students have problems not only coming up with material (because they're way too hard on themselves) but also keeping it going. That is, they find themselves playing a few notes and then stop cold because they don't know how to go forward.

The answer to this problem is similar to the approach just discussed. You see, you really aren't in "control" of the music so to speak. It has a life of its own and if you find yourself wanting to "push" the music out, you will run into blocks. This is called the principle of respect.

There are many, many times when I go to the keyboard to play and nothing comes out. It's frustrating! But, I know from past experience that if nothing wants to come at that particular moment, then I better get up and find something else to do.

Creating "Caverns" - an Improvisation Exercise

I created the piece "Caverns" using one chord. I'd like to explain how I accomplished this.

First off, Caverns is an improvisation exercise. Certain things I knew about this piece. One was technique. I knew that my left hand would just be playing an ostinato pattern using a D minor chord. My right hand was to play melody and bass notes.

With these decisions out of the way, the piece really created itself. I started by playing the pattern, then jumped in with a right hand melody. Then came the bass notes. These are played by crossing the right hand over the left but at no time does my left hand stop playing the ostinato pattern. This is really a unique little improvisation because it requires some skill in keeping the music fresh sounding. After all, I'm just using one chord. However, and this is important, the freshest sounding music will always come when the thinking mind lets go and the intuition is allowed full rein.

Once intuition takes over, the music that is created will always sound fresh. Why? Because it comes directly from the source. And this source also knows when to wind down. There is no ending planned out. The music winds down when the performer senses that it has played itself out.

Creating a Broken Chord Piano Improvisation

There are really only two ways you can play chords on the piano - solid or broken. While solid chords are nice, it's the arpeggio or broken chord that students love to play! Cascading notes shimmer and glide up and down the piano keyboard to create a waterfall of sound!

Creating a broken chord piano improvisation need not be difficult. All that you need to know is what chords to play and how to create the broken chord sound. Knowing the chords you will play is the easy part. Creating the broken chord sound can present some with problems. These problems can be easily overcome if we start out by using a special chord structure known as the open position chord.

Here, both hands are used to create a modern sounding seventh chord. The left hand gets the root, fifth, and seventh of the chord while the right takes care of the third and seventh as well. With this chord structure, the beginner can create that beautiful lush sound right away!

We can begin in the left hand and go up to play what is called an ascending piano run, or we can begin in the right and go down. We can alternate fingers back and forth to create different textures and use the notes under our fingers to explore a whole new world of broken chord possibilities.

For example, in the lesson, "Forest's Edge," we use open position chords in the Key of B Major to create an ascending broken chord run. Both hands are used to create it. The right plays melody notes as well. The amazing thing about this lesson is that it sounds a lot more difficult than it actually is to play.

Of course, broken chords can be played using triads, closed position chords, and any number of infinite chord varieties. But by using the open position chord first, students can quickly create a modern broken chord sound right away!

Creating a Free-Form Piano Improvisation

S o many piano students wonder, how can they improvise? They just don't understand how someone can sit down at the piano and play off the top of their head. What they don't know is, there is some method or system behind the pianist's approach. One of the best methods is to just pick a few chords from a key and play.

For example, imagine you're sitting down at your piano and you just want to play what you feel. What do you do? For starters, you could place your fingers on the first chord that calls out to you. Perhaps a minor chord is what you feel like playing. Or maybe you're in a Major mood. The key is to not think about it and allow the fingers to move towards what it wants. Take the lesson, "Reflections in Water," for example.

Here we start out by playing a C Major 7 open position chord. This chord choice really determines the way the whole improvisation is approached. By using this chord structure, you've already determined what the sound will be. Now, all you have to do to create your free-form improvisation is to play around with this chord and a few others from the Key of C.

In this lesson, you have the chords you will be playing and the order in which they are to be played. You can relax and play around with the possibilities and come up with your own unique improvisations. By using this lesson as a template, you begin to understand that the way pianists can sounds so professional when sitting down to play is by using chords.

Creating a Timed
Piano Improvisation!

Have you ever heard of a "writing prompt?" That's a tool creative writing instructors use to give students focus. For example, a writing prompt could be a photo of a beautiful nature scene. The instructor will then create an exercise where students write 1000 words or so about the picture.

The beauty of exercises like this is that it gives you focus! Focus to think of nothing but writing about and describing what's seen in the photo.

We musicians can do the same thing. We can use pictures, a descriptive phrase, or as in the lesson below, just a few chords. While the medium is different (music) the method is the same - get students to stop thinking and start creating!

The reason this works so well is you don't have to think about what materials to use. When we have four chords to play around with, we know the names of the chords and we know the chord type (open position.) Now all that's required is to sit down and just play.

We're not worrying if the music is "good" or "bad." We just play. And the more involved we get with this exercise, the more the music "loosens up." No thinking is required here. Just the ability to play around with chords and melody.

When the allotted time is up, we can either stop or continue playing. I advise students to stop playing when they feel themselves growing disinterested or bored with their playing.

The more you work with the power of limits, the freer your music will become. Why? Simply because you are not concerned with the outcome! Instead, your focus is on the process. And from this comes a music that is never forced or willed into being but one that is inspired right from the start!

Creative Piano Playing 101

So many piano students worry about playing notes correctly. They think about timing, dynamics, velocity, and so on.

Yet these same students are dying for the ability to feel something real. That spark of creative energy that enervates and refreshes the spirit.

Poets know of this feeling, as do painters and other creative people working in their respective fields. But what about music? Surely, we're not meant to spend months and sometimes years learning how to play other people's music. Yet, this is exactly what is being done in schools and universities around the world.

The piano is a marvelous instrument full of wonder. It sits waiting to be played. And you can play it! Not like traditional schools. You can sit down and let your fingers reach for a chord that calls to you. You gently rest your hands on this chord and music; beautiful wondrous music comes forth! How different this is than trying to play something someone else has written.

Your music is alive! It's unique and fresh and born of originality! Each note perfumes the air with delicate fragrance and you feel alive with this. Your heart and mind work together as the ideal music - YOUR MUSIC - floats into the air. The notes surround your heart and the hearts of others as they hear it. Gone is the need to recreate yet another dead composer's music. In its place, a feeling of quiet joy as you let go and let the music tell you where it wants to go.

Deep Piano - How To Go Beyond Surface Playing

All of us have our "special" times at the piano. You know what I'm talking about. Those times where every note sounds like it was meant to be and everything comes together. Body, mind, and spirit are aligned and the music that flows out of us seems to come from a limitless source.

Then there are times when nothing comes. These periods are frustrating yet essential to our growth. We may not like them, but unless we go down in the valley, so to speak, we will never see the next peak on the horizon.

I've found that it's best not to try and bypass this back and forth scenario. Some students get so frustrated that they try and force the music. This is a mistake and will only lead to further frustration.

The key to getting "back in flow" is to listen. Listening is essential for without it, we will only be playing on the surface. But if we tune in to what's going on inside of us - or more accurately, if we just let go and let the music itself speak through us, we're following our intuition and going with the flow rather than against it.

As you might have surmised, this is similar to meditation. Not the mantra chanting kind of meditation, but the kind where you just sit and allow thoughts to come and go... watching them go by as an impartial observer. Soon, thoughts slow down and we are left contemplating nothing. From this place can come your deepest piano playing.

To get to this place, it's a good idea to not have a goal when sitting down at the piano. You simply allow yourself to be and explore using the materials of music - chords, notes, etc.

Perhaps the key of G Major calls to you. Then, that is what you must play. Your intuition will never fail you and will reward you with some of the "best" music possible. You must release your grasp on what you want and allow for the unexpected to develop.

Easy Piano Improvisation: Learn to Express Yourself!

Have you ever wanted to just sit down at the piano and play what you feel? Without worrying if it's good enough or if you have enough "talent?" You can when you learn how to play piano using the amazing open position piano chord!

This chord structure allows the complete beginner to create modern sounds at the piano FASTER THAN ANY OTHER METHOD! After teaching piano for 14 years, I can safely say that I've never seen students progress as fast as they do when working with this chord position. Let's examine how one can improvise right away using the open position chord.

First, you must learn how to use it. The easiest way to do this is to simply learn the chords in the key of C Major. We take the entire 6-note chord and move it up step by step. First, we play C Major 7, then D minor 7, E minor 7, F Major 7, G 7, and A minor 7 and finally, B half-diminished. We play the chords first as solid chords (all tones together) then we break them up. For an excellent example of this, see the author's free piano lesson, "Reflections in Water" at quiescencemusic. com.

Once we've got this very large chord structure down in our hands, we can then use it to create music. Improvisation simply means spontaneous expression - learning how to create in the moment. Improvising does not have to be hard! Once you get the chords down, you're left with the melody creation aspect and this is easy to because all you use are the notes from the C Major scale.

We use our chords much the same way a painter uses a palette of colors. We create using chords and the element of time. In the example lesson, "Reflections in Water," the chords you play are in a given order. All you have to do now is play them in that order and improvise your own melody!

Easy Piano Improvisation Strategy Lets You Play With Freedom and Confidence

When I first started playing piano, I looked everywhere for information to help me play what I felt. And, much to my disappointment, I was left floundering in the library aisles.

One of things I'm good at is just knowing if something works or not. In fact, I can look at a book and within a few minutes, determine if it has anything useful in it.

It just so happens that during my library visit, I ran across a small book, barely 60 pages or so. This book contained nothing but chord progressions laid out over small 4 and 8-bar phrases. The goal of the book was to get you to play these chord changes and develop a sense of structure.

Well, it was brilliant. They say good things come in small packages and this was pure gold to me. I took the book home and started to play through the chord changes.

After all, here was something that was pretty easy to do. And it didn't require a lot of experience. Just knowledge of a few chords.

So what's the easy piano improvisation strategy here? Simple. You have to find the right kind of limits that will set your playing free.

You see, the problem for most students is not that they can't improvise. It's that there are way too many choices to begin with. By playing a few chords within a set framework, I learned that I didn't need a lot of material to begin creating my own music.

A great example of this is the lesson, "Reflections in Water." Here you have four open position chords to play. The chords are played in a certain order and music is made. It really doesn't have to be anymore complicated than that.

Five Minute Piano Improvisation - Reflections in Water

The idea that you can create a complete piano improvisation in five minutes seems undoable to most. After all, aren't you supposed to have years and years of theory and experience under your belt? Not if you follow this step-by-step video.

"Reflections in Water" is a piano improvisation I created to show students how easy it is to use something called the open position chord to create music. In fact, it's so easy all you really have to do is finger the chord and music comes out. How is this possible?

It all has to do with the way the chord is structured. Both hands are used right away to create a very open sound. This open sound is then used along with the notes from the C Major scale to create music.

We finger a few chords from the Key of C and we're off exploring a whole new world of sound.

The amazing thing about all of this is that most anyone can sit down at the piano, learn the open position chord, and begin creating music. It really is that easy. The only hard part at first is getting used to the wide chord structure. It really stretches the hands but once you get used to it, the rest is all downhill.

In the piano lesson video, "Reflections in Water," I begin by showing you how to play the chord up the C Major scale. I play the chord with each note being played separately. This is called broken chord technique and even this can sound musical.

After students get this chord structure down in their hands, the next part is showing them how to let go and allow the music itself to lead them. This is usually the hardest part for most students to get because they think they must force the music into being. But all that's really necessary is an attitude of exploration and play and the music begins to flow.

We play only four chords in this lesson. The left hand is locked but the right hand can be free to improvise notes from the C Major scale.

All in all, if you really want to let go and have a great time at the piano, learn how to play the open position piano chord.

Free Online Piano Lesson Shows You How To Improvise Step by Step

You ou want to learn how to improvise your own music on the piano. Most think this task is difficult. And it is, if you don't know what you're doing.

Fortunately, there is a way to actually improvise and create your own music at the piano without having to spend months... if not years learning how.

Take a look at the lesson, "Reflections in Water," (available at quiescencemusic.com). Here we have what is basically an improvisation exercise in the key of C Major.

You don't have to know anything about music in order to try this lesson. All you need is a keyboard or piano to practice on and the ability to stretch your hands out a little.

Step one of this lesson introduces you to something called the open position chord. This chord structure gives you the ability to play the piano with both hands right away. Plus, it's a modern sounding chord. This 6-note chord really stretches your hands and really is quite amazing.

The first thing you should do is get used to it and the best way this is accomplished is through playing it first as a solid chord, then as a broken chord.

If this chord type is new to you, you'll notice that your hands are being used to their fullest extent. In fact, you'll be stretching out over two octaves!

After you familiarize yourself with and play the chords you'll want to begin to improvise. And the cool thing about all this is that with this chord structure it's easy! All you have to do is create a little melody using the C Major scale.

The one thing that stops students from actually trying and succeeding at this improvisation exercise is the fear of actually doing it. If they would just take the first step and place their fingers on the keyboard, they would be halfway there.

Truthfully though, music instruction has, for the most part, dissuaded many from attempting anything like this. Most people think you have to have some extraordinary talent to improvise music. This belief has stopped many from experiencing the joy of improvisation. They think if they don't have the talent of a Mozart or Beethoven why even bother.

Nothing could be further from the truth. We try because

it brings us pleasure and that is quite enough of a reason to begin.

Free Piano Lesson, "Reflections in Water," Shows You How To Improvise!

I f you're like many who enjoy the piano, you've probably been mystified as to how someone can just sit down and play without sheet music.

It seems like an impossible feat. But there's a method to the mystery. **Pianists who can improvise know what they're doing and understand the fundamentals of improvisation.**

Now, if you're a newbie at this, it can be confusing to say the least! So many keys and so many choices! But you won't have this problem if you start out using a few chords and a way to play them.

For example take a look at the lesson, "Reflections in Water." Here, we have a lesson that shows you how to create your own unique music using just four chords. The chords are from the key of C Major and have a very "modern" feel to them.

To play this improvisation is quite easy. The first thing you need to do is familiarize yourself with these chords. Once you get them in your fingers and have committed them to memory - the rest is easy!

We now take these four chords and create our improvisation. We use chords, the scale of C Major and create with the element of time. These are our materials. Much like visual artists who use color and canvas, we musicians use rhythm, harmony, and melody to create.

We start out with the C Major 7 chord and notice that with this chord structure we get a modern sound right away! **No need to start with triads.** You can begin your study of piano improvisation with something called the open position chord and get creative quickly.

When you listen to the lesson, "Reflections in Water," notice that the music is quite slow. This is done on purpose. My goal was not to rush and come up with something sophisticated. On the contrary, my goal was to show you how easy it can be to simply finger a chord and create music. Something you can achieve if you put your mind to it!

Free To Be Creative at the Piano

I sometimes wonder why people even bother taking piano lessons. I suppose the hope is that one day, with a lot of practice, they too will be able to play Beethoven, Mozart, etc.

The idea of creating one's own music seems to be a foreign notion to most piano students. They believe it is beyond their ability. And with this belief they limit themselves. In fact, I think music may be the only area where **students are not encouraged** to be creative. Not only that, but the majority of piano teachers want you to learn how to note read before you learn how to play chords - that is, if they teach you chords at all.

You see, classical piano teachers can stretch their curriculum out forever. You could literally spend 10 years learning how to play other people's music. And while there's no denying this music is "good," it's also been played and recorded by people who have dedicated their entire life to getting it right.

Contrast this with visual artists. Do you think someone studying watercolor will spend years learning how to create another artists picture? **It's ridiculous right?** Yet this is what is done in the music world over and over again.

A student interested in learning how to paint in watercolor does not want to spend time learning how to paint the "masters." They want to be able to create their own beautiful paintings. So why should music be any different? It certainly isn't any more difficult than learning how to paint.

Personally, I have nothing against people who just want to play from fake books or learn the classics to perform for family and friends. I just wonder why the desire to create one's own music is so distant for most.

It doesn't have to be this way. Finding the right teacher or books is a start.

How To Quickly And Easily Improvise Your Own Unique Piano Music!

Improvisation... the word alone conjures images of free expression. It also intimidates those who have thought about actually trying it but stopped because of self-doubt. It doesn't have to be this way.

The ability to improvise music at the piano is a skill that, like most others, can be taught. For example, take a look at the lesson, "Winter Scene."

Here we have a basic piano improvisation using just two chords. The left hand plays a repeating pattern while the right improvises melody. It doesn't have to be any more complicated than this.

The problem most newbies make is they want to play sophisticated chords and elaborate melodies before they can play simply. They want to run before they can walk. And they soon talk themselves out of playing piano because it's just too hard or difficult.

The solution here is to just relax and play slowly. In "Winter Scene," you are asked to play an ostinato pattern and improvise your own unique melodies in the right hand. This is a perfect exercise for those new to improvisation because your task is so well defined.

You see, when you have too many choices you can get lost rather quickly. But if I were to give you an improvisation exercise that tells you to play these chords and this scale for a certain time frame, it frees you up! How? Because you now are no longer thinking of what to play. You know what to play. Now, you're only concern is with self-expression. **And once students get a taste of this, they always want more!**

It's very freeing, this ability to spontaneously create music. And the more one plays, the more one grows in this art. Not by constantly learning new techniques (although there's nothing wrong with this) but by turning within and listening.

How to Be in the Moment When Playing Piano

Your best music will always come when you are in the moment and just playing the piano. Why is this? Because you have forgotten about trying to make music. Instead, you are now "making" music. A subtle but crucial difference that can be detected by most careful listeners.

The key to being in the moment when playing piano comes when the technical aspects are mastered and the player can just play. Think of sports as an example. Michael Jordan didn't have to think about how to drive the basketball to the hoop. He had done it thousands of times. Now he could allow his intuition to guide him in making the best shot.

If Andre Agassi had to think about how to hit the tennis ball, he never would be able to get it to where he wanted it.

The good thing about New Age piano playing is that technique is easily learned. For example, in your free lesson, "Reflections in Water," you have four open position chords to play. Once the technical aspects of playing these chords is down, you are free to allow your feeling to guide you in making music. Now you are "in the moment" and can let the music tell you where it wants to go -not the other way around.

How to Improvise Freely On Piano!

Ah, to sit down and play. One of the joys of being able to play the piano is to know how to play it. But so few can or do. What I mean is this - if you can't walk over to your piano, sit down and just play whatever you feel, you are shortchanging yourself on a wonderful experience. Plus, it's not as difficult to do as many might have you think.

The thing that stops more students from being able to improvise freely is self-doubt. They just don't believe they can do it. And of course, they lock themselves with this belief. I can relate. I had to work long and hard to give up my own set of self-limiting beliefs about what I could or couldn't do on the piano. One of the biggest of these was "I'm not good enough."

This thought in particular will freeze you and keep you stuck. Look at it this way. No one is good enough! That's right! No one will ever be the best at playing piano because there will always be someone better - technically speaking that is. That's why it's very important to free yourself from such inane beliefs. Listen, you are good enough and you are ready to express yourself at the piano. Here's one method that will have you improvising freely in no time.

We'll begin with the piano lesson, "Reflections in Water," as an example. It's a free lesson that everyone has access to. The beautiful thing about this lesson in particular is that you are given a way to play the chords that sound modern and you are given the chord progression to play. You are free to create your own melodies to these chords. You see, another thing that students often don't get is that you need a set of limitations to improvise freely. Why? Because there are so many choices!

By giving you a certain key, chords, and chord progression to play, I'm limiting your choices so you can focus on expressing yourself rather than trying to decide what chord to play. Eventually, when you understand how limitations work, you'll be able to create your own set.

Now, with these parameters in place, we can sit down at the piano and spontaneously create music!

How to Improvise Using a Few Chords

When a painter is getting ready to paint, a color palette is usually chosen first. For example, if a forest is to be painted, the artist may choose browns, greens, and blues for the sky. Once the palette is chosen, it makes it easier to create the painting. Why? Because color decisions are now out of the way.

We can apply this concept to music as well. In particular, New Age piano playing. In your lesson, "Reflections in Water," we have four chords to play with and we have the order in which they are to be played. Now, all that is required "to paint" your sound portrait is the ability to take these chords and play around with them.

Once the decision about what chords to play and how to play them are out of the way, you can now focus on making music. This is how I created Reflections in Water. I knew that the piece would be in the key of C. I then chose a few chords from this key and fooled around with them.

It can be very confusing for the beginner in improvisation. There are so many choices and ways to go about making music. This is why limiting choice is important. Also, it is equally important to begin by using simple means. Many students think that if they can't compose like Beethoven or Mozart, they are untalented. Get rid of this idea quickly. Everyone starts from simple means and it's a good idea to begin your experience in improvisation the same way.

How to Improvise a Complete Piano Piece Using Just 2 Chords!

Most people think you need to learn sophisticated chords and lots of them to play "good" piano music. Wrong! You don't need to learn hundreds and even thousands of chords you'll never use. What's perfect for the beginner and experienced player, too, is to limit choice!

Just a few chords, a scale to improvise in, and we're off creating a world of sound! For example, take the lesson, "Winter Scene." Here we have two chords played by the left hand. We use a certain pattern to play these chords with and we've created a harmonic background. All that's left to do now is to add in the melody (foreground) and that's it - an improvisation that can last as long as the improviser is in the present moment and the music remains fresh.

The beautiful thing about limiting choice is that it gives you focus. You don't have to think about how many chords to play what chords to play, etc. Instead, you can focus your creative energies on improvising melody. What a difference this approach can have for newbies at improvisation!

No longer trying to master technical aspects, they can actually enjoy the process of being in the moment and creating spontaneous music. So many people think they can't do this because they're scared they don't know what they're doing or that it will sound bad. All excuses! By jumping in the water and starting out EASY, a complete beginner can start enjoying the great art of improvisation.

How to Make Your Boring Piano Improvisations Come to Life!

Do you think you need to constantly learn new techniques to become better at piano improvisation? Do you believe that getting one more technique under your belt will make you a better player?

Nope. Not going to happen.

If your piano improvisations sound boring it can only be for one reason. It's because you're bored!

It's not the piano or the chords you know or any one of a hundred different things you tell yourself you need before you can sound "good" on the piano. No. The problem is not with technique or chords. It's with you.

Listen to this - if you're bored when playing the piano your mind is elsewhere. When this happens the music that comes out of you will reflect this. It won't have that quality you want it to have.

The solution is to BECOME AWARE of your mental state. If you're bored or your mind is on other things, simply acknowledge this silently and refocus on the music. If this doesn't work, get up and move on to something else. Your piano isn't going anywhere. You can always come back to it later.

Look, I know how frustrating it can be when nothing is happening. You want to play. You feel like playing. But nothing is coming out. You're bored, frustrated, and upset. You may even think the creative muse has left the building. The truth is, there will be those times.

If nothing is coming through, forcing it won't work either. There are those who suggest you stick with it until you come out on the other side. This may or may not work. Just remember not to work against yourself and your piano improvisations will come to life when you are truly present with the music.

How to Play Like George Winston

George Winston is the poster boy for New Age piano. There's no denying this. And why not? The man practically put New Age piano on the map with his CD, "December." So poignant, so sad and filled with joy is this music, that it resonated with millions across the world.

Many years ago, I read an article where George describes what he does on the piano. He said something like; "I get my left hand down. It's like the band and has the bass and chords. Then the right hand is free to do its thing."

Now, George Winston didn't invent this technique, but he put it to good use in creating unique atmospheres for piano. In lesson forty, "Flashflood," I illustrate what George does best, namely, get a very nice background going with the left hand while the right improvises a melody. Using only two chords, we can create a aural canvas upon which we "paint" our melodic portraits.

The trick is to get the left hand down well enough so you can freely improvise with the right. Now, the hard part of this is being able to "freely" improvise. This requires much practice and it is a very good idea to take it slowly and build up to a freer right hand.

How to Play What You Feel

Many students think that being able to play what you feel is difficult. They believe you must have years and years of training in improvisation and theory.

The truth of the matter is that playing what you feel is easy when you understand what feeling is. Feeling is not emotion, yet it contains emotion. For example, if I'm in an ecstatic state of happiness and rush over to the piano and play, what I am doing is tapping off of the emotion.

To play what you feel does not require high or low emotional states. On the contrary, feeling is always with us and to just sit down and play is all that is required. Our feeling is what comes out of us in the moment. It lies in wait but is always there. Think of freewriting as an analogy. To put pen to paper and just write what comes to mind, the writer is expressing feeling. Emotions may come up during this process, but they gradually return to the pool of feelings from which they came.

To play what you feel requires nothing more than being present at the piano and having a little skill in being able to improvise. For example, in creating lesson #35, "Moss Garden," certain decisions were made in the beginning. The sound was determined (pentatonic). Chords were chosen and a technique was chosen too (broken chord).

With these decisions out of the way it becomes a matter of playing around with the possibilities. And from this playing comes a music that is not forced or willed into being. On the contrary, feeling is allowed to be expressed normally and naturally. It becomes an easy thing to do, just like freewriting.

How to Stop Thinking and Start Playing

Learning how to improvise is confusing for most. The sheer number of choices becomes a burden. Should I play this note? What chord next? Where do I go from here? All valid questions newbies (and oldbies) at improvisation sometimes ask themselves.

The number one reason people have problems creating in the moment is that they won't let up on themselves and just play. They knew how to do it once as children but now that memory is gone and with it, a void has taken its place.

Fortunately, there is a solution. It's really a two-pronged solution because once we do learn how to ease up and just play, we are left with another problem and that is, what game are we playing?

The game of improvisation is a game like any other. We have a few rules, some guidelines, and then the game is played. You see, we must have some kind of structure to play the game of improvisation. Why? Because without it there would be way too many choices and this would prevent most people from even beginning.

Here's a perfect example. In Lesson 5, "Winter Scene," we have two chords, a scale, and a way to play these chords. With these choices out of the way, we can now focus on and enjoy the act of improvisation. We can play around with the music and feel good about our play.

Some think working within a set of limitations is uncreative. I thought so too once, until I realized that unless I learned how to do this by following the examples of others, I couldn't be free to create my own set of limitations.

How to be Creative at the Piano

You want to be more creative when playing piano. Many students wish they could just sit down and improvise their own music but don't know how to begin.

They think if they can't play a fugue like Bach, they are untalented. Or, they think the music that comes out of them must be sophisticated or it's not worth anything. Fortunately, there is a style of piano playing that bypasses this academic snobbism and allows the beginning (and advanced) student to be more creative.

The New Age piano style is geared towards improvisation

and creativity specifically because it requires very little in the way of technical know-how. What it does require is the courage to just sit in front of the piano and allow for the creative act; allow being the important verb here.

Many students wonder why they have problems improvising. When I explain to them that the problem is not with technique but attitude, they look at me surprised. After all, aren't they willing to learn? Of course! But they must first shun the "creative genius" persona and be willing to let go and let the music tell them where it wants to go.

Once students understand that they aren't in charge of creating music, they begin to have that knowing inward smile. They have discovered that the secret to being creative at the piano is to release all expectations of good or bad and focus on the process. Then they can relax and fully enjoy all that music has to offer.

Improving Your Improvisation Skills

What exactly is improvisation? It's a word that means, "to make up," or to create without forethought or plan.

Many students want to improve their ability to improvise, but make a big mistake when they think this means learning new techniques. No. The key to improving improvisation skill is to be able to let go of the need to control what comes out of you and let the music itself takeover. This makes all the difference!

Here, we are not making something up or trying to produce something. We are allowing the music to come through us and be born of its own. This "difference in approach" makes all the difference because it puts an end to trying to come up with material! Being able to improvise does not mean having a lexicon of techniques to draw upon. It does not mean virtuosity at all. It means being open and receptive to what's coming next.

This skill is developed as you learn how to accept what is coming out of you, regardless of so-called mistakes or errors.

Your improvisation skill will increase with your ability to relinquish control. A paradox to be sure, but one that I've found to be true again and again. Learn technique, of course. Learn chords, yes. Then, let it go and play the piano.

Improvisation Practice

In her book, "*Writing Down the Bones*," Natalie Goldberg talks about writing practice. It's an exercise where you sit down and just write without editing what comes out of you. This is also a good idea for musicians to do.

She'll have her students complete timed writing exercises, i.e. you sit down and write for 20 minutes non-stop. Your job is not to critique the writing but enter into it like a meditation.

The whole purpose of this is to get to a place where you are not thinking - you are feeling. This is the realm of true artistic expression and can be reached by anyone if they learn to let go of self-judgement and instead, focus on the process of creating.

The most fun I have is when I let go and just let the music

take over. It's only at these times that I'll write something down that resonates within me and develop it into something later - which is not to say that it is not something already.

In Tibet, the monks have a tradition of creating elaborate artworks out of sand. They may work months on completing it. Then when they feel it is done, they will destroy it. A nice way to keep things in perspective.

They realize that the creating was what was most important, not the beauty of the finished product.

Improvisation and Musical Form

D o you ramble on endlessly with your improvisations? If so, good. This has its place in music making and in new age piano playing in particularly. Just listen to New Age pianist, Michael Jones's music to hear an example of this kind of free-form improvisation.

Now, some of you want to create something that will give the listener a slightly more cohesive experience. How is this accomplished? By forming the music into a shape - an ABA shape for our purposes here. To give form to music does not require as much theory and technique as most people think. In fact, it is as simple as applying the principles of repetition and contrast.

In most new age piano music, there is some kind of form that the composer uses - whether it's extended "A" form ala Michael Jones, or extended "A" extended "B" and back to "A" again, as in some of George Winston's music. Think in sections, people. A section of music can last for as long as the person who created it is involved with it - that is, as long as the inspiration is fresh.

As soon as the music sounds dull, it's time for a change - the next section of music. This is the point where a composer will add something - new (contrast) or, if she is smart, end the piece. If the music does not have that freshness, that touch of inspired in the moment fantasy, you'll be able to detect and hear it. Some composers are so in touch with their feeling that they can take you on a 20 or 30 minute journey using very little means, but by using the elements of repetition and contrast maintain listener interest.

First, get your "A" section. The first few bars (eight, usually) is more than enough to propel you forward. You must adopt a listening attitude to hear what is coming next. You don't force nor will it into being. This will not give you what you want, which is, I'm assuming, inspired content. Listen, listen, listen and the music will come. If it doesn't, just do what Beethoven did.

He worked on 3 or 4 pieces at a time. When the inspiration dried up on a particular piece he was working on, he just moved on to another and picked up on the others later on. You can do the same. Be bold and go forward. Be afraid of not trying. Don't be afraid of making mistakes.

Improvisation is About Feeling

t really doesn't take much to improvise. A few chords, a scale to play in, and that's that. But once these technical decisions are out of the way, we must allow our feeling to guide us.

Playing this way has many advantages. First, you don't have to worry about what you're going to play. You let your intuition guide you in this. The hands are placed on certain chords. The fingers move and the mind is in abeyance, waiting in surprise to see what the hands will discover.

You also don't have to think about what chords to use or how you're going to play them. When you take care of the technical aspects first, you free yourself to explore your materials. Of course, things can change and we must allow for this, but playing within a set of limitations will free the mind.

For example, in the improvisation exercise, "Monterey Beach," two chords are used. How they are played is determined and a key is chosen. Now, the improviser can relax and explore the possibilities available.

The other way of playing, the way where there are too many choices present, distracts the improviser from improvising. The mind must be free from these distractions so feeling can be expressed easily. Many students have a problem with doing things easily.

Instant Piano:
A Quick Tip For Creating Great Sounding Improvisations!

We all want quick results. And fortunately for fans of the New Age piano style, quick results are easy enough to obtain.

One of my favorite techniques for creating a great sounding improvisation is to use something called an ostinato pattern. The reason I like this technique is because of the variety available. There are literally millions and millions of combinations.

For example, in the lesson "December Twilight," (listen to it by clicking below) we have a left hand ostinato pattern. The amazing thing about this is that it's just 2-bar repeating pattern! And only two chords are used -A Major and D Major. With just this small amount of material, a few minutes of music is created.

If I wanted to "extend" this piece, I could simply add in another ostinato pattern and this is exactly what I did in the following lesson.

You see, many students have a problem because they think they have to come up with something "sophisticated." They believe you must have complicated patterns that stretch the hands and challenge the technique of the player. But if you just want to relax, have fun and create a simple heartfelt music, you don't need all that.

All you need is a few chords and a simple ostinato pattern. With this in place, you use your right hand to improvise with. Here's a secret for you -improvisations using an ostinato pattern really rely on the right hand to make it sound interesting. For instance, one piano player may be able to play for a minute and come out with a fresh sounding improvisation. Another may go on for 5 minutes or more.

It really all has to do with being in the moment and just playing. So, to come up with a great sounding improvisation, just create a simple ostinato pattern in your left hand and let your right have fun creating the melody!

Keys to Successful
Piano Improvisation!

L et's get right to it. What is the one factor that will have you playing the piano freely and easily?

It's not technique. Most students can learn the technical aspects of piano playing extremely well and still sound wooden and lifeless. In fact, the most technically advanced students can sound extremely sophisticated when you hear them. The quick as lightning runs - the facile arpeggios up and down the keyboard - may dazzle the ear but...if the playing lacks spirit, the music will suffer for it.

It's also not theory. Knowing how to produce counterpoint or advanced harmonic techniques also won't make you a good improviser at the piano. It has nothing to do with this at all!

THE SECRET IS...

So what is it? What makes one student sound like the music is ethereal while another one sounds like a robot performing? It's your ability to let go and allow the music to tell you where it wants to go!

I've said it before many times but it bears repeating. As soon as you try to control the outcome, as soon as your ego thinks it can create a "good" music or a "better" music, the X factor slips away.

The reason it's so important to allow the music to lead you and not the other way around is simply that you are tapping into a source greater than you are. And this source will give you music far superior than anything you could have come up with on your own.

RESPECT YOUR MUSE

Bach, when asked how he could compose so much music responded this way, "My dear sir, I have to be careful that I don't trip over the music when I get out of bed in the morning." In a sense, he was saying that he really had nothing to do with the creative output. He was allowing the muse to lead him.

Another amusing anecdote comes from Beethoven. When a violin player complained to him that he couldn't play a certain passage because it was way too difficult Beethoven responded, "Do you think I worry about your lousy fiddle when the spirit moves me?"

This is a perfect example of respecting your muse. Beethoven heard something and wrote it down. He wasn't thinking about the technical aspects of what was coming through him. He was being respectful to his muse. By the way, by doing this, by being respectful of your muse, you will discover things you will never have been able to discover any other way.

So the secret to successful improvisation is just to let go of your need to control the outcome. Then, and only then, will your true music come to the surface.

Learning How To Improvise

Those of you who have been reading my articles for some time now know that I believe improvisation to be the cornerstone of musical creativity. Why? Because without the ability to just play, we become stifled and the "real" music that is within each of us withers and dies.

Now, if you're a writer, you have lots of support in this area. There are books, (many, many books) that explore the topic of free writing to its fullest. There are plenty of exercises and advice from professionals in the field. There are even classes designed to "free the writer within."

But what about music? Where can the aspiring piano improviser go to get help and advice on this topic? Traditionally, they would turn to Jazz - a word synonymous with improvisation. Jazz is a big believer in learning scales and chords. In fact, there are 1000's of scales and 1000's of chords to learn. This can be a turn-off for the beginning student who simply wants to dive in and express through music.

Learning how to improvise need not be difficult. There are only 2 things required:

The ability to trust your intuition
Knowledge of a few chords

Learning a few chords is the easy part. The part that gives more students problems than anything else is getting over perfectionism and the fear of making "mistakes."

I remember when I first started playing the piano. I wanted very badly to "create" something. Little did I know that by wanting so badly to create, I was blocking the creative impulse. You see, we must learn to play first! Very hard for many adults, because they want to make something "worthy" of performance. If they only would ease up a little and relax and not worry so much about what was coming out of them, then they would begin to experience the joy of improvisation.

Monterey Beach - An Improvisation Exercise

Hearing is believing. Most people can't believe that you can only use two chords to create a few minutes of music. They really can't believe that they can do it themselves on the piano. Here's where the fun begins.

For instance, take the improvisation exercise, "Monterey Beach." Here, we use only two chords, A Major 7 and F# minor 7 to create a nice little improvisation.

Because we know that we will be playing just two chords, it allows us to move around with them and express ourselves at the keyboard much more easily. Why is this? Because we've limited choice. You don't have to worry about when to switch chords or what chords to play. The improvisation exercise takes care of that. Now, you can just focus on playing around with your materials, in this case, chords, and have fun.

This approach to improvisation gives students the opportunity to relax and actually enjoy the process of music making. They don't have to worry about scales or practicing for hours on end in order to "sound good." On the contrary, students learn that they can actually play the piano using chords and make music right away!

Improvisation exercises like "Monterey Beach" prove to be an invaluable way for students to understand how to use the materials of music - which are chords and the element of time. We play around with these two and are surprised at what comes out of us. Perfection is not our goal here. Being in the moment and experiencing the joy of improvisation is.

Music Without Goals

really love improvisations that go nowhere. Improvisations where there is no goal... just an impulse to follow feelings in the current moment.

In fact, some have described this kind of music as self-indulgent - a kind of musical fantasy world where the focus is more on the performer than the listener.

Of course, this isn't the case at all. You see, most of us are used to having our music wrapped up in nice neat little packages. We aren't used to actually listening to music. We expect an "emotional experience" right away. And it better happen in 3-4 minutes or else.

Take Japanese Shakahuachi music, for example. For those of you who don't know, the shakahuachi is a Japanese flute. It's beautiful sound is appreciated by many in the East.

I have a few CDs of this music and everytime I listen to them I hear something new. It's as if each time the CD is played I hear it for the first time. It never gets old. Why? Because of the absence of musical form!

There is not much for the mind to grasp or hold onto. Repetition of musical phrases is almost non-existent. Instead, we get music without goals!

If there is a goal at all, it's that the person performing the music remains in the present while playing. What we hear is the "state of mind" of the performer at the exact time the recording is made.

In one of my own piano pieces "Cirrus," (listen to it at quiescencemusic.com) I do the same thing. And every time I listen to it, it seems that it's somehow changed. Yet the music always remains fresh and pliant - waiting to be discovered again and again.

Having said all of this, I have nothing against musical

form and the works that come from it. I just think the "other" kind of music is just as valid and important.

New Age Piano and Improvisation

There are so many areas in life where one must do things right. Thankfully, art is an area where great discoveries are made by making mistakes!

Take improvisation for example. We sit at our piano or keyboard without any thought of what is to come. Our fingers touch a certain chord that calls to us and we are gone. We are transported into a nonverbal world where anything is possible.

Surprises happily come our way as we let go and observe how the music is created before us. And we are always amazed that the "best" music happens when we do not care if it is good or bad.

We are not concerned with good or bad but with feeling and music alone. We allow ourselves to be wrapped up in this world of sound and it does transform us. When the music has played itself out, we rest and notice that the world seems a little lighter than it was before we sat down to play. Not because of anything we did or did not do. But because we let ourselves relax and become co-creators of the music. We improvise for the fun of it and for the enjoyment it brings to ourselves and to others.

Piano Chords For New Age Piano

If you like the beautiful sound of New Age piano you're going to love this.

Listen... most of you know what triads are. These three note chords have been the essential building blocks of western music for at least four centuries.

One thing about them though.... They're outdated!

Of course they're still used. But there's absolutely no need to start with them. Instead, why not begin your study of piano chords with something called the "open position" chord.

This chord structure gives you the freedom to play with both hands together right away! Plus, it's a modern sounding chord.

The thing that frustrates more students than anything is what they're playing. Usually constrained to ancient textbooks that teach triads and scales, the hapless newbie plunges ahead in the hopes of eventually playing the piano. The catch here is two-fold. First, when you do eventually get to play music, it's that of other composers. Sure... the music is good. There's no denying that. But it's not modern. And it's not your creation.

Secondly, if you follow these textbooks, all you'll be able to do is read music. You won't be able to create it on your own.

With the open position chord, you can begin creating your own unique music right away. Take the lesson, "Reflections in Water," for example.

Here we have four open position piano chords along with the order in which they are to played. Once you familiarize yourself with this chord position and get it under your fingers you're ready to explore! These modern piano chords are perfect for the light, airy New Age piano style and will have you playing the piano in no time at all!

Piano Improvisation - Easier Than You Think!

As someone who has played the piano for quite a long time, I can tell you that there is nothing more enjoyable than being able to sit down and just improvise.

I don't do this every day, but when the mood strikes I do. It might be a beautiful spring morning, or the sight of something inspirational, but when the feeling comes, I move towards the piano and just play.

I take for granted that I can do this because I've been doing it for a very long time. It's now a part of me, and a part I would never want to give up or lose. Now I know that some of you may think only a few gifted individuals can do this, but let me tell you that IT'S ONLY IMPROVISATION AND THIS CAN BE TAUGHT!

You don't need much to begin. Just a few chords under your fingers and you're off exploring a world of sound. Once you begin to improvise and experience for yourself how easy it can be, it becomes addictive. You'll find yourself wanting to play the piano more and more. That's why I'm not a big fan of routine practicing.

I believe that students will play the piano when they see how it can benefit and enrich their lives. Then, they will naturally want to play. In fact, it may be difficult to pull them away from playing.

I'm also a big advocate of keeping it very simple in the beginning and focusing more on cultivating a productive attitude in the student. One thing I've learned from teaching piano for the last 14 years is that students who don't believe they can improvise won't be able to. This is the biggest road-block students have in the beginning.

But once they see that they can improvise and create music on their own, the rest is usually easy.

Piano Improvisation Journeys - Create Your Own Unique Music!

There's something about being able to just sit down at the piano and play. Especially when the music isn't planned. We allow ourselves the freedom to just be at the piano and wonderful things begin to happen.

To create your own piano improvisation journey, you need to know a little about chords and how to play them. That's pretty much it. I never understood why teachers make their students wait so long before they can dive in creatively at the piano. Especially since all it takes is giving students the right kind of limits so they can freely express themselves.

For example, in the lesson, "Reflections in Water," you have four chords to play around with and you have a way to play them. The lesson is in the key of C Major so it's all on the white keys. The chords are learned, practiced, and then the student is allowed to explore these materials and see what comes up.

Explore is really the idea here. Too many students want

to force their way into improvisation. It really is all about attitude here. I can't think of a better quote to illustrate this than, "In the beginner's mind there are many possibilities, in the expert's mind there are few."

It really is true and it's also a good thing, because it means you don't have to be an expert to experience the joy of piano improvisation. On the contrary, the freshest sounding music can come from someone who does not have years of theory and training under their belt.

In fact, you can, if you listen closely, hear the mindset of the person playing. Some have no problems emptying themselves at the piano and can allow the music to take them places that they've never been before. These "journeys" are precious for they really are inroads into ourselves.

To take your own piano improvisation journey remember that's it's not about how much you know. It's really about how willing you are to let go and let the music itself take over.

Piano Improvisation Tips - Enjoy the Process First!

"I'm having problems staying with the music," wrote one student. "I can't seem to get it. What I mean is, I get stuck or blocked only after a few seconds of improvising. What can I do?"

The above complaint is a very common problem among newbies at improvisation. They don't understand how to keep an improvisation going. Why? Because they have it backwards!

You're not supposed to keep an improvisation going. No. That's the wrong approach to improvisation. The right approach is to let go of your need to control the outcome. Then, and only then, will your intuition come to your aid.

You may want to create something beautiful on the piano, but your desire is creating blocks! How? Because the ego wants a perfect music, a good music, or something that will satisfy it. The ego is insatiable and is never satisfied.

That's why when you focus on and enjoy the process of improvising, you free yourself from this trap.

Many of us are obsessed with creating a product. Something we can be proud of and show off to friends and family. Look, there's nothing wrong with wanting to have something you can call your own, but when you are only concerned with creating the end result, your creative self (inspiration) will dry up and leave you feeling empty.

But, if you put process over product, not only will you enjoy the whole experience more, the outcome will be far superior to any forced ego product you may end up having.

To enjoy the act of making music, we must let up on ourselves and adapt an attitude of exploration. We must allow for mistakes and listen for where the music itself wants to go. This idea may be strange to some of you. I can understand that but once you really let go of trying to control the outcome, wonderful things begin to happen!

Piano Improvisation Using Left Hand Ostinato Patterns

Did you know that one of the easiest ways to get into piano improvisation is by using a left hand ostinato pattern? This is because the ostinato takes care of the harmony aspects. Now all you have to do is improvise a right hand melody.

The cool thing about ostinato patterns is that there are literally millions of them! That's right! You can experiment with the time element and come up with something unique every time you sit down to play. Of course, those of you who have been reading my articles for some time know that I don't suggest you try and come up with something. The best way is to just play!

For example, in the lesson, "Giant Sequoia," we have a lefthand ostinato pattern that uses 2 chords - A minor and F Major. We use the entire left hand spanning an octave and we've created a nice harmonic backdrop where we improvise our melodies. The key of the piece is A aeolian. This is a minor modal scale and gives the piece a somewhat sad, yet poignant sound. The right hand is improvising thirds. With these "limits" in place, we can focus on the task of improvisation. I must say that it can be easy to get sidetracked.

We all want to create something, but what most don't realize is that wanting to create really stifles the creative impulse. I say this not to undermine those who want to compose and create their own music. I say this because it's true! The ego always wants to take credit for whatever it comes up with. But remember that it's only when the ego is bypassed that your "best" music will surface.

Pure improvisation without thought of outcome is the best practice you can have for allowing the music inside you to come out unfettered. That's why lessons like "Giant Sequoia" are worthwhile. You can actually have fun without worrying if it's good enough!

Piano Meditations: A Beginner's Guide to Playing What You Feel

I f only beginning piano players realized that they could create their own unique music right away, perhaps more of them would.

What I mean is this...most students, young and old alike know only two ways to learn piano. The first way is the classical route. Here, note reading and playing of the classics is taught.

The second way is playing pop standards from either fake books or fully written music sheets.

That's it! That's what most people think of when they're considering learning the piano. But, it doesn't have to be that way at all. For instance, if you only know two chords and the notes of the scale or key these chords are in, then that's all you need to simply BE at the piano.

Imagine allowing the music to just flow forth from your fingers. There is no thinking involved. No forethought of what is to come. Just a simple act of sitting down and playing. This method of piano playing is completely foreign to 99 percent of music students. Even Jazz, which is seemingly all about improvisation, requires a much more rigorous and thorough approach.

Instead of taking months or even years to prepare yourself to play piano, I suggest a complete attitudinal change.

What I'm talking about is radical, yet will make perfect sense as soon as you read it and it's this:

DON'T MAKE THE MUSIC MORE IMPORTANT THAN YOU ARE!

What do I mean by this? Simple. Most musicians have a lot of ego and want people to praise them and tell them how good they are. Now, there's nothing wrong with a little ego stroking, but music can give you as much as you are willing to let go and allow. This simply means that you let up on the need to control where the music is going. Instead, you allow the music to guide you to where it wants to go!

I know this sounds like mystical wordplay, but think about it and you'll see that I'm right. You see, the problem most students have is that they think they need to learn a lot of theory before they can be any "good" at the piano.

They also think they have to be "good enough" before they even attempt playing piano. These beliefs are sure to stop you dead in your tracks. You are more important than the music, which is to say... who cares how good or bad it sounds. The real question is are you enjoying yourself. If so, then you are way ahead of the game!

Piano Music, Perfectionism, and Self-Expression

Is your heart in the music? If so, it won't matter what you play so much as what is received through your playing. Do you still think you need to learn 43 chords to sound good or are you concerned with the joy of expressing yourself through this wonderful instrument called the piano? People who sound like they know what they are doing may indeed know what they are doing but does that mean you want to listen to the music?

Let's look at pop music, for example. Here is a music that is produced so tightly and carefully that nothing is left to chance. Not a crackle or hiss, not one static spot on the entire three to four minutes of the track. Yet after a few listens or even after a single listen, the mind may grow disinterested.

It's like a sporting event - exciting and enthralling while you are there but once over let down and perhaps even a little depressed. Now most (but not all) pop music is like that. It gets you hooked up for a few minutes, gives you a feeling, usually of excitement, then its gone. New age music on the other hand is a more sincere and heartfelt expression, and as such, mistakes are allowed.

I'd like to share something with you. When I recorded both "La Jolla Suite" and "Anza-Borrego Desert Suite," I made mistakes. "La Jolla Suite" was recorded live so I couldn't help that, but the Desert Suite was done in one take. I wasn't so concerned with the production value as the emotion I felt at the time I was playing. I could have gone back and redone the tracks I didn't like so much, but then I could have gotten stuck in a perfectionist's rut.

No, I decided that a "wrong" note here and there wouldn't kill what was heard and might even make it sound more authentic. So if you hear a mistake, it may sound like I don't know what I'm doing. Perhaps not. But that doesn't concern me. What concerns me is one thing and one thing only - am I present at the piano? Am I there in spirit as well as body? If so, I am doing what I'm supposed to be doing.

Reflections in Water -
A Piano Improvisation Exercise

I n the piano lesson, "Reflections in Water," you learn how to use a few chords and the C Major scale to make music with. But how is this accomplished? Through the power of limits!

You see, when you know that you'll be playing only four chords, and you know how to play those chords, it frees you up to focus on making music. You're no longer focusing on the technical aspects of playing the piano. On the contrary, the technical aspects have been taken care of. Now you are free to explore the tones under your fingers and to experience the joy of music making.

In the beginning, when you first start playing the piano and trying to improvise, you may be overwhelmed with the amount of choices you have. In fact, the choices you have are astronomical! That's why limiting choice is so powerful.

The first thing to remember is you don't need a lot of material to make music with. A few chords, a way to play them and a key to play in are all that is required.

Many students fight the idea of limitations thinking that it constricts creativity. Nothing could be further from the truth! All artists work within either prescribed or self-imposed limits and you can save much time by working with them, not against them.

Successful Black Key Improvisation

What a great instrument the piano is - white keys, black keys, and 88 tones make it incredibly versatile! Most students take it upon themselves to try and master this instrument. They begin to learn note reading and go through a series of books before they are ready to play the music of the masters.

If only they realized that a world of free improvisation was waiting for them on the black keys, they too could experience the joy of improvisation right away. They might even forget about note-reading for a while and actually enjoy themselves as actual music was being made.

For example, take the lesson, "Oriental Sunrise." This is a black key improvisation based on the E flat minor pentatonic scale. Now, when most people hear the term "black key improvisation" they think of children banging on the piano creating some kind of noise. And while this has its place, the adult can create quite a beautiful sound by using only the black keys.

The secret is in how the keys are played. Anyone can go to the piano, sit down and play. The keys are there and are readily accessible. However, one person may just plunk around while another is able to create music. It's all about sensitivity! The sensitive musician is able to create music using only a few notes. The non-musician can not. They have to learn to get in touch with themselves first.

If you can go to the piano, play a black key improvisation, and make it sound like music, you are way, way ahead of the game! You understand that it's not how many notes or chords you know, it's how they are played that makes the difference!

Taking the Mystery Out of Improvisation

A student recently asked me; "Why is improvisation so mysterious?" My response was that there is nothing mysterious about it at all.

Of course, I'm saying this because I have years of experience under my belt, but truthfully, once you understand that all you need to improvise is chords, the mystery disappears and satisfaction takes it place.

Most of the problems students have with improvising is their fear of trying it. They think they need to know college theory or advanced harmony first in order to begin creating in the moment. Nothing could be further from the truth! In fact, extensive knowledge of harmony and theory can actually create more problems than they solve.

For instance, in one of my piano lessons, lesson 3, "Rainforest," I have two chords down in my left hand. I then use the G Major scale to improvise a melody and that's that! Nothing hard about it. No mystery here - just fun!

Once you have a definite exercise to play and know what your hands will be doing, it frees you up to create. You no longer have to worry about which chords to play or how to play them. You can focus your attention on the act of improvising melody and experience the joy of improvisation!

The Freedom To Explore
At The Piano

Many of us are afraid to experiment with music - to branch out and see what's out there. This is understandable. Most of us were taught to follow instructions carefully with the hope that one day, we too would be able to play the piano.

Something is missing isn't it? Some important ingredient most music teachers simply don't know how to teach.

Listen... what you're missing isn't technique or the ability to play well. Both of these can be taught and are being taught to students on a daily basis. What you're missing is freedom. Specifically, the freedom to explore and experiment on your own at the piano.

Children know how to do this. In fact, it's hard to stop them from doing it. They don't understand what "wrong" or "bad" is. Their only interest is in exploring and finding out what pleases them.

It's no wonder that adults who still retain this child like quality are called geniuses. You see, they simply refuse to surrender their joy to someone's expectation of what "good" is.

And why should they? When you make art - any art more important than yourself - you make a critical error that can take years to correct.

Allow yourself the freedom to explore. To make mistakes. To make a mess. To play the piano without worrying if it's good enough.

The paradox to this approach is that music created this way almost always sounds better than music that is created from an "ego" perspective.

The Joy of Spontaneous Expression

Do you remember finger-painting as a child? How fun it was? How exciting it was to be able to dip your fingers into a color that called out to you and put it on paper! The excitement of it all came from the feeling that you were an explorer, looking into uncharted territories of your own creative source.

Now music can be that way too! All that is necessary is to understand that you don't need any special talent or ability with which to create music. Two chords are enough to begin experiencing the joy of spontaneous expression. In the lesson, "Oriental Sunrise," we have two chords to play around with. And two chords are more than enough to create music.

The problem that most adults have is the ability to relinquish control. They want to be able to make decisions and direct the music to where they want it to go. And of course, they lose the ability to create. Why? Because they believe they must make decisions as to what notes to play, what chords, how fast, etc. It can be very threatening for some to allow for "mistakes."

Many adults feel that they must be perfect. It is this perfectionism that destroys the spirit and stops any creative impetus dead in its tracks. The solution to all of this is to remember the finger-painting child within each of us. Each of us knows intuitively what colors call to us the most. The key is to be able to trust that intuition, and let it guide you!

The Key to Creating Fresh Sounding Piano Improvisations

Some music just has it. You know the kind I'm talking about. The kind of music you can listen to over and over - and it never gets old.

So, what's the secret? How can music remain fresh after multiple listens? I'll tell you. The secret is the performer was in the present.

You see, music is an instant transmission of feeling. Whatever "mental state" the performer is in while playing can be detected by careful listening. That's why some performances, although technically correct, lack feeling or emotion. The performers' mind was somewhere else.

The key to creating fresh sounding improvisation is to be in the present while playing. But, this is more difficult than you think. Our minds are always busy. Thoughts skitter back and forth while we're at the keyboard and if we are improvising, the music coming out will reflect it.

The best way I know to stay "in the present" while playing is to just play! This may sound overly simple but I assure you that the attitude of play is very important.

Think of children drawing with crayons. They are only interested in the joy that comes from putting color on paper. The marks and scribbles are just reflections of the child's inner state. And while most children's drawings look horrible to the average adult's eye, they do say a lot.

Music is really no different. We take a few chords and play around with them. We improvise and see what comes up. If we remain in the present, the music that comes from us has a magic quality that is hard to define - but you know when it's there.

Remember, process over product. The big mistake many

students make is that they want a finished product they can show off to others. There's nothing wrong with this and it's natural to want to share our creations. But we must decide which is more important... our own joy and happiness at the piano, or the approval of others.

And by the way, it is possible to have both.

The Most Beginner-Friendly Way to Improvise

Most students try too hard. They really want to be able to improvise and to sit down at the piano and express through music. But, they try too hard and miss the point of it all. It doesn't have to be that way. In fact, improvisation should be a joy. If it isn't, you are doing something wrong.

Here's a simple method to get you going. Look at lesson 3, "Rainforest." Here we have a strategy for successful improvisation. The left hand takes care of the background while the right is free to create whatever it wants from the G Major scale - an excellent method for beginners.

The key here is to forget about the left hand ostinato pattern and shift your attention to creating melody in the right. Once you get the pattern down your focus should be on melody creation. What's great about "Rainforest" is that you only get two chords to play in the left hand; something beginners can accomplish easily. But here's where some students get stuck. Why? Because they play something beyond their technical ability and either lose the left hand pattern or stop playing because they don't like what they're hearing.

Here's a secret - go as slow as you need to. There's absolutely no need to be a speed demon here. The goal is to make music, not show off and see how "well" you can play. Go slowly and play with sensitivity. Here's another bit of advice - the sensitive player will ALWAYS SOUND BETTER than the player with technical proficiency.

It doesn't matter if all you know are the notes from the G Major scale, but, if you play with sensitivity and feeling, you will sound better than the musician who knows everything there is to know about music!

The Secret to Fresh Sounding Improvisations

I once had a student ask me how to improvise for more than a minute or two. He had some trouble keeping the music going for longer periods of time.

I told him that the problem wasn't with knowing enough material. He already knew how to play a few chords. It was his attitude - that the trying to come up with something was what was blocking the creative flow. This can be hard to understand. After all, aren't we supposed to "come up" with something? Isn't that what invention is all about? In a word - no.

Being present is the key to allowing the music to unfold. Blocks happen because we are not present to the moment.

The minute you start thinking of anything else (actually, the minute you start thinking) is when the critical voice comes in. Improvisation is spontaneous creation within limits. Successful improvisations don't happen out of thin air.

Certain decisions are made AT THE BEGINNING. For example, I may find myself playing a D minor chord. This may happen completely at random with no prior decision being made. I can, in fact, gravitate towards a particular sound. However, as I am playing this chord, I look down at the keyboard and it occurs to me that this is a D minor chord. I know that if I start with this chord I could play an improvisation in the mode of D dorian. I have all the chords of this mode to use.

Now the game is an improvisation in the key of D dorian. I could stray and go into different tonalities, but I have made a preliminary decision that the improvisation will be in D dorian. This frees me up by allowing me to focus on just a few chords. Now, I can play for as long as I like.

There is no secret to keeping an improvisation going. Keeping it sounding fresh is another thing. I could play for hours if I wanted to using just the chords in the D dorian mode, but, I think I would want to stop playing when I became bored.

The secret to fresh improvisations is always to let the music tell you where it wants to go. You need to step out of the way and allow the music to happen.

Top 7 Don'ts for Successful Improvisation

1. Don't try and make something happen. Trying blocks the creative flow and will result in blocks.

2. Don't expect to create something good. Expectations will always come with judgements and consequently, you'll end up feeling let down.

3. Don't worry about what is "coming out." Improvisation is about play and freedom to explore. Abandon unrealistic expectations and experience the joy of improvisation.

4. Don't try and please others. The first person you must please is yourself. This may seem obvious but don't underestimate the strong need to please - ESPECIALLY WHEN IT COMES TO THE ARTS!

5. Don't try and accumulate a "lot of knowledge." All it takes to improvise is a few chords and the proper attitude.

6. Don't think. Improvisation is about FEELING. It's about being in the moment and experiencing the moment through the music. Thinking will take you away from your intuition, which will guide you if you listen to it. Intuition will lead you places thinking never could!

7. Don't quit. Practice is what makes intuition stronger. The more you practice or play, the stronger your intuition will grow and the more you will trust it. Your unique voice will emerge and will grow stronger each time you sit down to play.

Top 7 Do's for Successful Improvisation

Do you think you can't improvise? Nonsense! All you need are a few chords, the right attitude, and a piano or keyboard. Follow these seven principles and you'll be improvising at the keyboard in no time!

1. Do listen to what's going on inside yourself before and while you sit down to play. Your inner state will determine the emotional quality of your playing

2. Do let go of the need to be perfect. Trying to "be correct" will defeat the playful attitude necessary for improvisation

3. Do believe that you are good enough to begin. No one person knows it all so you might as well jump in and experience the joy of improvisation.

4. Do realize that you don't need a lot of theory or technique before you're ready to play piano in the new age style. If you don't begin now, when will you?

5. Do understand that improvisation is not some mysterious skill, but a game that can be learned and played just like any other game

6. Do enjoy the process and let go of the outcome. Trying to control what comes out of you is a sure way to stop the creative flow

7. Do stop playing when you become bored or indifferent. There is a natural starting and stopping point to playing. Just like anything, when you feel yourself growing disinterested, stop playing.

What Works Best in New Age Piano Improvisation

Many students want to know how to improvise. What they really want to know is how to be able to keep an improvisation going.

It's not difficult to begin. You just play a chord or two and that's that. But what happens to many students after a few seconds is they don't know what to do next. They get "stuck." Why? Because they are thinking about what to play. Wrong approach!

For example, in lesson 12, "Coral Reef," we have two chords, A minor and F Major. And with these two chords, music is made. This improvisation lasts for a few minutes but could have gone on much longer.

You see, what works best in New Age piano improvisation (or any improvisation) is for the person improvising to be in the moment. This is most easily done when the technical aspects are taken care of (i.e., only having two chords to play) and letting go of the need to control the outcome.

Think of building a sandcastle as an example. Children love to build sandcastles. Do they spend years learning how? Of course not! Once they know the fundamentals, they forget about how to do it and focus on the pleasure it gives them. Most adults wait too long before diving in. They're scared that they will fail and discover they have no talent. But talent is not the issue - you're sense of joy and discovery is!

Why Learning How to Improvise is So Important

Imagine asking a beginning writer to write a short story from scratch. Our writer does not yet have much experience in writing but accepts the challenge and begins to plunge ahead.

He has to start somewhere, so he begins to examine how to construct a short story. He learns all about plot, character, and structure and now believes he is ready to begin writing.

As soon as he begins to write, he discovers something. He can't move forward. He is blocked. What's the problem? He knows how to construct a short story and should be able to forge ahead right? The problem is he has not allowed his "voice" to unfold naturally. His internal critic is blocking the natural voice inside his head and the pen stops cold. What to do?

Our writer must learn to freewrite so words can flow freely and not be stopped by the editor voice. The same principles can be applied to us as musicians!

We may want to compose our own music and we may also know all about how to do it, but unless we are able to improvise freely and allow our own natural "voice" free reign, the music stops and we lose the ability to move forward.

This is why learning how to improvise is so important. It allows us to move forward! This benefits us in two ways. One, we begin to understand that the joy of music making itself is its own reward. Second, we begin to trust our voice and feel confident in our ability to move forward without judging the "quality" of the music.

You Can Create Your Own Music - Even If You've Never Touched a Piano In Your Life!

A few days ago I was going through some student emails and one question really popped out at me:

"Edward, I really want to just sit down at the piano and improvise but I don't think I know enough to begin. Can you help me?"

Here's my answer to this student:

Dear P.,

There are really 2 issues going on here. The first is the belief that you don't know enough. The second is the idea that you need to know a lot in order to begin. Let's deal with the first issue -the belief that you don't enough.

Many students share this belief. They think they need to understand a lot more than is necessary before they take the "plunge" into improvisation. The truth of the matter is they're actually scared they might be able to do it after all... and that would quickly eliminate their belief that they can't.

This seems strange but it really has to do with fear of the unknown. Many of us can do things we previously thought were impossible -and are impossible -unless you actually give it a try!

The real stigma has to do with thinking that what you're producing isn't good enough. Because if you truly didn't care about the outcome, your focus would be on pleasing yourself first and enjoying the process -something so many adults wish they could do, but are reluctant to do for fear of creating something "bad" or "unworthy."

I always tell students that it's far more important to actually enjoy yourself at the piano than to create something others can approve of. Some have an extremely hard time letting go of the need to gain others approval and this itself can cause a lot of anxiety and needless striving.

All you really need to begin improvising are 2 things:

Knowledge of a few chords
Willingness to take the plunge

After students begin to improvise without worrying about whether the music's good enough they begin to tap into their own creative source. When this happens, a small miracle has occurred. Once you actually taste how good it feels to let go and allow the music to move through you, it becomes addictive. Then you'll want to play the piano more and more. And the more you play, the more you learn. Not by accumulating knowledge but by allowing yourself the freedom to explore.

Edward

You Can't Force Play

A student once asked me; "How come sometimes the music comes freely while other times, I feel blocked and can't play?"

A perfectly valid question and one that many students of improvisation ask. The problem is that many think they should be able to just sit down at the piano and play anytime anywhere. But this is unrealistic. Why? Because you can't force play!

Improvisation is play. And when you try to force the music to appear, the exact opposite happens. Blocks to receiving the music are set up and the spirit is let down. All this can be avoided if we learn that there is a certain ebb and flow to creativity. Respect this natural tendency. Learn to see the creative force as one that naturally goes away, only to come back again, stronger and revitalized!

There is a natural order to creating that, if respected and trusted, will serve you well. Listen to yourself and don't let your ego get the best of you.

Many students fear that if they can't go to the piano and play, they're creativity is dried up. Not true! They may be experiencing an ebb tide period. During this time, it's best to take a break from playing and come back later on when the creative waters return.

Learning

Adult Piano Lessons - How to Begin

You're not 10 anymore and you want to learn the piano. You're not alone. Many adults would love to take piano lessons but don't really know how to go about it.

The first thing you as an adult should ask yourself is "What do I want to learn?" Do you want to play in the classical style? You're in luck because there are literally thousands upon thousands of teachers specializing in this area.

Do you like Jazz and want to play the piano this way? You're in luck again! Many teachers specialize in only jazz piano and you can find these instructors by picking up your local Yellow Pages.

What about contemporary/New Age styles? Unfortunately, there aren't too many options available to you here. Especially for New Age piano, there are teachers who can help you learn how to create your own unique music, but these are few in numbers. Fortunately, we have the Internet! You can learn how to play piano online!

It's not as far-fetched as it may seem. The idea of having a private teacher who can look over your shoulder and correct your mistakes and guide you is beneficial in may ways. However, many adults like to work at their own pace and learn on their own. That's why the Internet is an excellent starting point to discover the many offerings available to you.

Online adult piano lessons offer you the opportunity to learn on your own terms, but make sure that you can talk with an instructor if you need to. Also make sure that the lessons include audio and that they are easily understandable.

Beginners Piano Lessons Should be Exciting

What is it that a beginner at the piano wants to do? They want to make music! It might be classical, jazz, or something else, but one thing is for sure; they don't want to spend months studying boring theory.

What if instead of studying note reading, beginners piano lessons were focused on the student actually learning how to create music? Just imagine the excitement when the notes and chords played are all original and express what is actually being felt.

I don't know why piano teachers start their students off on note reading. It's boring, unnecessary for most students, and really doesn't help the student create anything at all. In fact, you could say that by learning to note read, students are speaking the language of music without really understanding the underlying grammar and syntax -which has everything to do with chords!

Chords are where the excitement lies. And when the beginning piano student starts to play chords on the piano, it naturally leads to music making.

Beginning guitar players don't have the same problems as

newbie piano players. They expect to be able to create something that sounds like music immediately. This isn't to say that learning the guitar or any instrument does not require serious study. It is to say that one need not spend thousands of hours learning note reading while the world of music is only a few chords a way.

Beginners piano lessons should be exciting! They should inspire students to want to study the art of music further. They should be easy enough where the beginning student is not easily discouraged.

Computer Piano Lessons And Why You Should Consider Taking Them

We all want a good deal. There's no denying that. Yet many would be piano players are missing out on some amazing deals online. Specifically, I'm talking about computer piano lessons.

The technology has finally enabled many offline teachers to put their materials online via video and audio. In fact, thanks to sites like YouTube and Google Video, students can actually watch instructors perform the lessons.

And the best part about these computer piano lessons is that many of them are free and are available right now. Just visit YouTube and type in the phrase "piano lessons" and the number of results that pop up will amaze you.

In fact, if you're interested in learning jazz piano, there are a few jazz videos available. Like New Age piano music? The author's own videos are available teaching this style of playing.

And let's not forget about price.

The average cost these days for quality piano instruction runs anywhere from $30 to $60 an hour or more! There's absolutely nothing wrong per se with "live" instruction. You can get instant feedback and have your progress monitored. But, you can now have the same scenario online without having to pay an arm and a leg for it.

Last I looked, most computer piano lessons were no more than $30 to $50 for a full month! And that's the high end of the spectrum.

The way it works for most online piano lesson sites is that you pay to get access to a library of lessons. The benefits here are very real. For example, you can work at your own pace and review the lessons over and over again - something you can't do with a live instructor. Most piano courses also have a message board so you can also "talk" with the instructor if problems or questions arise.

All in all, taking computer piano lessons is a good deal and one that should be investigated.

Creative Piano Instruction - Does it Exist?

When most people think of piano lessons, they think drudgery. Beethoven, Czerny, scales, etc. What most people want, however, is to be able to express themselves creatively.

It's a fact that if you decide to learn how to play in the classical style, you can pretty much forget about creating music. Instead, you'll be recreating works that were inspired centuries ago and bringing them to life.

This is fine for most people and the curriculum usually stops here for them. For those who aren't satisfied with this routine, there is very little in the way of creative music instruction - except for jazz. In jazz, you learn theory, harmony, etc. But even here, it is suggested that you really not attempt anything creative until you get enough technique under your belt.

Then there is New Age music - my favorite genre. Why? Because it is heartfelt, yet not sanguine. It is honest, yet not sappy. In short, here is a music that is contemporary, likable AND EASY TO LEARN!

I'm always amazed that teachers want to start their students with repertoire that dates back as far as the 16th century. While there is no question this music is "good," it's also dead. While a beginning writer who wants to learn the art of fiction will read the best authors of the past, he or she also wants to create something modern! Something that has their own voice. Why should music be any different?

Piano lessons don't have to be the dull, lifeless exercise we know they can be. They can actually be FUN!

Creative Piano Lessons for the Absolute Beginner

You've been thinking about taking piano lessons. And you're a beginner. You probably think you'll begin your piano lessons studies with note-reading and triads. And you'd be right!

Most piano teachers begin their students out on some obscure method book that drags out the teaching process. This makes your piano teacher rich and you a much poorer piano player.

You may be thinking there's a better way to learn piano. And you'd be right again! Listen to this. What if there was a method... a way to play piano right away using a modern sounding chord? And what if you could use this chord to create your OWN music instead of playing Kum-ba-ya 40-50 times for practice.

You're in for a treat because this kind of piano instruction exists and can be found right on the Internet. I'm talking about something called the Open Position Piano Chord. With it, you can quickly and easily create your own unique music. Not in months or years. Not even in weeks. I'm talking about hours!

But how you ask?

The answer is easy. The Open Position Piano Chord uses both hands right away to create a modern sound. Once you master this chord position (takes about 10 minutes or less) you'll be well on your way to playing contemporary styles. The best part about this chord structure though is how easy it is to create with.

Because both hands are used immediately, you have the opportunity to play with the tones under your fingers. The lowly triad, while still used in much western music, is not so friendly in this regard.

With the triad, you get three tones to play around with and while you can create some music with this, it's just not what today's sound is all about.

The Open Position Chord however gives you a modern seventh chord to play with right away. Used in Jazz, New Age, and Contemporary styles, the seventh chord is the foundation of most of today's music!

If you want to get really creative at the piano, try the Open Position Piano Chord and you'll see how your piano lessons will become that much easier!

Edward Weiss's Piano Playing Secrets

I've been playing the piano for over 14 years now and I've learned a few things that help me stay focused on what is important to me when sitting down to play. Following in no particular order are three "secrets" I've discovered:

Secret #1: Only Play What you Love

For those of you who don't know, I play and teach New Age piano. I don't play classical or jazz. Not because I don't like these styles, but because when I sit down at the piano, the New Age style is what is inside of me. Of course, I could play classical and jazz, but I just don't want to and neither should you if that's not the style you're interested in. If you play what you love, technique and growth will naturally follow and you will tend to spend more time at the piano than away from it.

Secret #2: Learn How to Improvise

I never understood the allure of playing other people's music via note reading. Now, don't get me wrong - some of the best music in the world was produced centuries ago. But, and here's the interesting thing, Beethoven, Mozart, and Bach were all excellent improvisers. That is, they could sit down at the keyboard, finger a chord, and produce music. Of course, these great composers learned from others and could read music but I can almost guarantee you they viewed the art of improvisation to be important - not for the listening public, but for the performer so he/she could get in touch with their muse.

Secret #3: Listen for Your Tone

You know what's amazing? I'm always getting better at playing the piano by listening for my tone. Here's what I mean. I play a piano key. A note sounds. Many times I'll play sloppily and not really hear the sound that is being produced. Tone is very important because it determines how sensitive a player you are and sensitivity is the hallmark of artistry. Any clod can sit down at the piano, hit a key and produce a sound. It takes the artist's touch to get a beautiful tone. I learned about tone by listening to my favorite piano player, John Herberman. Each note is beautifully played and sensitively interpreted. If you think playing slow pieces of music is easy, try playing a very slow piece and really listen for the tone you're producing. That's a good litmus test.

George Winston and David Lanz - Learning How to Play Like Them

Did you know that there are two styles of New Age piano playing? One style is more percussive and staccato ala George Winston. The other, much softer and quieter. You should learn both styles! Why? Because there are times when you want to really "bang on the keys" so to speak and other times when a gentler mood takes over. Let's explore both styles and see how they're created.

First, the George Winston style. When Winston came on the scene in the early 1980's, he introduced the world to a new piano style. His debut album December (still widely ordered today) put solo piano back on the map. His style, though varying throughout his career, is a percussive one, especially for new age piano. Using left hand ostinato patterns, Winston then improvises/composes melody on top.

His style was so popular that many pianists, including myself were influenced by it. To play in the Winston style, hand independence must be learned, because it's the left that sets the background. The right then comes in with improvised melody. The easiest way to learn this is to practice simple ostinato patterns first. When a pattern can be kept going in the left hand while improvising freely in the right, you're on your way.

New Age pianists David Lanz and Michael Jones made the second, softer style popular. These two pianists focused more on soft textures, especially Michael Jones. His music is usually one extended improvisation. Lanz focused more on melody. To play in the Lanz style, it's good to know how to create or compose a melody because this is what he leads with. To do this, you should know about musical phrases and how they're constructed.

Get Piano Lessons Right on Your Computer!

You want to learn piano. Yet you're finding the fees a little hard on your wallet. No problem. Now you can get piano lessons online!

It's a lot easier to do than you might think. Learning how to play piano usually requires a live teacher and some kind of instruction book. But thanks to the Internet, you can still get the teacher (although not completely live) and the same kind of instruction - but at a fraction of the cost.

During these tough economic times, it makes sense!

Now you may be wondering, that sounds good, but how will it actually work? Good question.

Thanks to sites like YouTube and Google Video, you can now see the teacher teach. This is an amazing advance and one you can take full advantage of. For example, a teacher can give a complete lesson illustrating techniques and procedures on video. In addition, he or she can write down what you ought to learn.

This is really no different than what a "live" teacher does. You have a certain curriculum, you have goals that your teacher sets for you (homework) and then you follow up your teacher on a regular basis.

The same thing can be done online! Most online instruction sites have forums and/or message boards where you can actually "talk" with your instructor and other students in the course. This beats driving or walking to see your local piano teacher.

Now, let's talk about the dreaded fee. Most piano teachers today charge anywhere from $40-$60 per hour or more. After a few months, that can add up. In a year's time, you might even break the $1000 mark.

For many, this is worth it and I would say that that's true. However, many adult students don't want or need to learn a classical repertoire. They're more interested in just playing and expressing themselves on piano. For these students, the Internet is perfect!

Good News for the Musically Untalented

Have you ever been told that you were good at something, but not good enough to make it a career or life ambition? Especially with music, if your passion is music, you are hopelessly outnumbered right from the beginning. "You better have a back-up job" or "Don't put all your eggs in one basket" are common refrains heard from well meaning adults who inadvertently had their dreams crushed out of them.

The world has more then enough computer programmers and engineers and these professions are well paying ones. What are we musicians to do? Well, for one thing we can forget about needing "talent" to make it. What is talent anyway but a person's ability to connect with his or her audience. You might think that talent means technical proficiency. You couldn't be more wrong.

Here's the good news. Connect with yourself and your art and you automatically become talented. This means you don't have to wait years and years before you begin to share what comes out of you with others. In fact, most so called "really talented people" last in the limelight for a few years or so and then burn out to non-remembrance. If you consider yourself hopelessly untalented, you are focusing on the wrong problem.

The question isn't, do you know enough. The real question is, are you confident enough to believe in your own abilities. If you do, you will go far. If not, there's not much hope. Those who are able to let go and connect with the music inside of them are already truly talented.

How a "Difficult" Piano Student Actually Showed Me How to Teach Piano

'll never forget the time I was giving lessons to this one student. Talk about difficult. She just couldn't get it. And the "it" I'm talking about is not reading music or playing Beethoven or Bach. I'm talking about improvisation.

No matter what I showed her she just froze up.

I then realized something. This student really wasn't having problems getting the technical aspects down, i.e., chords. The problem was she didn't think she could do it! <u>It was all attitude</u>.

I then had a lightbulb moment. If the basic problem with most adult students is not technique but attitude, then I had to come up with a different approach to reach them. And that approach turned out to be mentoring.

What people really need is to believe in themselves. If

this aspect is missing, no amount of technique or theory will help. In order for me to be helpful, I had to act as a therapist so to speak... <u>gently guiding students to believe in themselves</u>!

Once they could do this, the rest was a piece of cake. Look at it this way, if you don't believe or have the slightest faith in your own abilities in anything be it writing, painting, whatever, your chances for success are slim indeed!

To help these "shaky" students, I used basically a two-fold procedure.

First, they needed to relax and not worry so much about what was coming out of them. Performance anxiety can happen even when we play for ourselves. The critical parent shows up even when we're playing alone. I had to help them overcome that critical parent first.

The second prong was simply to build up their confidence by showing them how easy it could be to create once that critical voice was eliminated. They watched me play and saw that I didn't care if I made mistakes or if the music was "good enough." My mentoring allowed them to see that the joy of the process was far more important than any product they could come up with.

How to Make
Your Piano Playing Come Alive...
Without Using Any Hype!

Have you ever listened to your favorite pianist and wondered why their music felt so alive? What was it?, you wondered. Was it technique? Maybe, but probably not.

Technique can allow you to play difficult passages. It can't give you the "X factor" that careful listeners can discern.

Perhaps it was the personality of the performer that drew you in. Personality is great but will only take you so far as a pianist. After all, if they can't see you, it's just the music that's heard.

So what is it? What is it that makes one pianist sound alive while another sounds like they just don't have it? You may think it's how much someone has practiced or how many years of conservatory is under the belt. It's none of these. The best players, the ones whose music has something otherworldly about it, have relinquished control of their egos and allowed their higher source to take over and guide them! That's it.

They may not say it, but if you notice, the best players never take full credit for their playing. In fact, most players at this level will say nothing unless pressed to. You see, once the ego is out of the equation, the player is free! And once free, the music is allowed to flow and move through the player as if... yes - as if it is something coming from another world - or at least a higher place.

To make your piano playing come alive, you must let go and allow the music to take over. I know I keep saying this but only because it's true. As soon as you think that you are a good player, or even a bad one, you're setting yourself up to fall. Certainly, it's OK to have a healthy does of self-esteem and admit that you feel good about your playing but...

Here's an interesting tidbit. Do you know why Mozart only wrote first drafts and never scribbled anything out? It's because he trusted himself so much that he knew that his first drafts were the best ones. That is, he learned to get out of the way and let the music speak through him.

How to Play Piano
Using a Few Chords

How many chords do you need to create a piece of music? Would you believe that it doesn't really matter and that whole pieces of music have been created using just one chord? For example, if you play a D minor 7 chord, you could use the bass note D to create a drone effect and anchor the whole improvisation. It could last for a few seconds or many minutes.

The important thing is were you in the moment when you created it? If you were, then it will be a good piece of music. If you weren't, it will be notes in the air without communication. What communicates is your feeling. It's your feeling that gets across through the notes. The notes themselves are meaningless if you are not present behind them.

I usually do not use more chords than four or five when creating. I use the chords of a certain key, for example A major and stay within that key until the piece is done. I may change to a different key, but I will always begin with the intention of staying within one, always keeping the possibility open for change. Remember the power of limits, especially in music.

When you have too many choices it can be overwhelming and will stop you from being able to go forward. That's why learning to play in 4 and 8-bar phrases is important. It gives you the limit of chord changes. New age music is mostly a static music meaning that the chords do not change too much. In fact, you can have the same chord going on for 8, 16 and even 24 bars or more. The amount of change is dictated by personal taste and that you will acquire after you freely experiment with the music.

Remember that attitude is the number one thing. You must allow the music to tell you where it wants to go or you will most likely freeze up and stop the forward momentum. That's why I always tell students the principles for creativity must come first. Without that you are really starting on shaky ground.

So, don't worry about how many chords to insert in your music. For a good example of chord changes, look at my book, "New Age Piano Made Easy." It's filled with 84 exercises completely comprised of different chord changes in all 12 keys.

How to Play Piano in Less Than One Hour!

I f you're looking for a way to quickly play the piano you're going to love this. Listen... most of you already know that the quickest way to play the piano is by learning chords.

But what most of you don't know is what kind of chord to start out with. There are triads, seventh chords, diminished chords and thousands more. There are closed position chords and then there is the open position chord, and with it, you'll be able to create your own music in less than an hour!

The reason why so many people have problems with the piano is <u>they give up out of sheer boredom!</u> They sense that it will take months if not years to create something that sounds like music on it. So they give up.

By starting out with open position chords, you'll immediately sound like a pro! Why? It all has to do with the way the chord is structured. First, it's a modern sounding seventh chord. All this means is the seventh note of the scale is used to along with regular triad notes to give it a more contemporary sound. Jazz musicians use it all the time.

Second, it covers more than two octaves of the keyboard giving you a very nice "open" sound. If you love contemporary stylings, you'll be playing them in no time with it.

And last but not least, you use both hands right away to create with! In fact, the chord is so wide open that you can literally create music without moving your hands around at all.

If you love the idea of playing piano but don't want to start with boring triads or note reading, you're going to love learning to play the open position chord!

Keyboard Lessons - Simple, Fast, and Focused!

When most people think of taking keyboard lessons, they already have a certain style in mind. Classical, Jazz, Contemporary, New Age... all these styles are available to learn.

The problem is, most students, especially adult students don't want to wait months or even years before they can play something that sounds like music. Especially with the classical style, students are expected to master note reading and do everything "correctly" before they are allowed to play something creative.

And what they do end up playing is usually a piece that was written way before their grandparents were born.

<u>The solution to this is to learn a chord-based approach first!</u>

What do you think Bach, Beethoven and other classical composers used to create their music? Chords! They knew how to compose certainly, but by using chords, they were able to think creatively and quickly block out entire sections of music.

You don't need many chords to begin with. Just a few to explore the world of music. One chord position I'm fond of, the Open Position Chord, allows beginning students to create a modern sounding seventh chord and use both hands right away. It's really a great way for students to begin their study of chords.

Think of guitar players as an analogy for music making. Do they begin their study of the guitar by learning how to read music? Usually not. I say usually because classical guitarists have to read music but in every other genre - rock, jazz, finger style - chords are what is emphasized. Students choose the style they want to play in, then find teachers or books that give them instruction on how to construct chords on the guitar. They're also taught how to create chord progressions.

Within an hour or so, the beginning guitar player is creating their own music! Piano lessons can be the same way. Of course, teachers can and do teach a chord-based approach to playing the piano but they can make a lot more money by dragging students along for years as they read notes and play other peoples music.

If you want something a little less daunting, start by learning chords. It's simple, fast, and a very focused way to learn the piano!

Learn How to "Speed Listen" in a Few Easy Steps!

Most of you have heard of speed reading That's where people skip and skim through the written word to get to the "gist" of the material. But did you know you can also learn how to speed listen? That's right!

You see, the key to speed reading is reading "for something." That's it. That's the entire key and once you understand this, you'll understand how people can literally flip pages of a book and seem like they're covering vast territories. Yet all they are doing is searching for information they want.

For example, let's say you have a non-fiction title you want to speed read. How to do it? First, before anything, you ask yourself "what information am I looking for?" By asking yourself this, you bypass "read mode" and instead go into "search mode." Of course, it helps to skim the table of contents first, but after that, you can find the info you need fast because you know what you're looking for.

We can also apply this concept to listening to music. For example, let's say you're listening to a Mozart piano sonata and want to know what's going on. How do you do this? Easy. You listen "for" something. In this case it might be he harmony, form, how he uses dynamics, etc. Do you see how this can help you? By deciding what to listen for before hand, you become a search engine ... literally listening and waiting to hear what you've decided to learn.

Let's take a concrete example. In my YouTube video, "Piano Therapy," we have a short piece of music lasting a few minutes or so. Now, suppose you want to know what the form of this piece of music is. How can you quickly determine this? Easy. By listening for the form.

To do this, you must **pay attention to how the composer uses the tools of repetition and contrast to construct his music.** In this case, the form of the music is a simple ABA. You can go further. You can listen for the arrangement of the piece or how many times the composer repeats certain sections. If you want, you can take pen and paper and write it out as you listen. I used to do this to discover how music I liked was constructed.

You can listen for introductions, transitions, and modulations... pretty much anything you want to learn. The key here is to determine what it is you're listening for and then do it.

Learn Piano Fast - Even if You Don't Know Where Middle C is!

You want to learn how to play piano. So do thousands of others around the world. Here's how they usually go about it.

First, they try to find a piano teacher close to where they live. They may or may not know what style they want to learn, but figure the piano teacher can help them figure this out.

Next, it's off to the piano teacher for the first appointment. What usually happens here is the teacher gives the student "an assessment" to see what they know. Now, for the most part, piano teachers won't ask prospective students what they want to learn because they assume it will be classical in nature.

The benefits for the piano teacher in teaching the classical method are enormous! First, students must learn how to read music and this can take anywhere from one month to one year depending on how fast a learner the student is. Second, students learn classical repertoire and this can literally take forever. As this is happening over time, the student becomes a piano player who can read sheet music and play the music of dead composers reasonably well. That's the goal anyway.

The student at this point may have spent thousands of dollars learning how to do this thus increasing the piano teacher's income. What a great deal for the piano teacher! <u>But what about the student?</u>

If your goal is to learn how to note-read and play other people's music for fun then that is what you should do. But if you're interested in a more creative approach to piano playing, you may want to seek out a teacher who will show you how to play piano using a chord-based approach. Here's why:

Time spent learning is greatly reduced. Listen to this... you can learn most chords on the piano within one month's time. You won't be an expert at it, but you'll know enough to get around on the piano. This puts you light years ahead of your classical playing counterparts.

Musicianship is quickly realized. Do you know that most classical players don't have a clue how what they are playing was created? That's right! They just play the notes like a typist and never understand the mystery behind the music. Now, if you learn chords, inevitably, you're going to learn about chord charts and once you learn how to "chart out music," you'll be thinking like a composer. You'll be quantum leaps ahead of most classically trained musicians.

If you really want to learn how to play piano fast, learn a chord-based approach first. You can always learn note reading later on.

Learn Piano Online and Save Time

Do you know how long it takes to learn the piano? Well, depending on the style you're interested in, it could take up to 10 years! That's if you go the classical note-reading route.

But, if you want to learn piano online the easy way and save yourself years of struggle, <u>learn a chord-based approach first</u>. Sure, note reading is the way most teachers suggest you start out. They reason that you need to read the language of music before you can actually play or create it on your own. Wrong! You don't need to learn note reading to play the piano. All you really need is knowledge of a few chords and how to play them. And this information is readily available online.

No more writing weekly checks. No homework or punitive teachers over your shoulders here! Indeed, <u>the great benefit of learning piano online is that you can learn at your own pace on your own schedule</u>. The time you save can really add up; not only in hours but in dollars as well.

For instance, let's say you decide to see a "live" piano teacher. The average rate these days are between $30-60 per hour. Let's say you're charged $40 an hour and you see a teacher every other week. After 1-year, your total cost comes to $1040.00!! That's a lot of money to learn how to note read (which, by the way, can also be learned online.)

Now, let's say you decide to learn piano online for $9.95 a month. That comes out to just $119.40 for the entire year -and that's with full access to many lessons that you can access anytime you want. Quite a difference! And that not only results in saved money, but saved time as well!

Learn and Play Piano Now With This Easy to Use Technique!

You want to learn piano and play it now, but you don't want to spend years at it. Understandable. You're going to love this. It's something called the ostinato technique and with it you'll be able to improvise and create your own unique piano music right away!

An ostinato simply means repeating pattern. It's used in all types of music and is perfectly suited for the piano. Why? Because it's easy to create with! For example, let's look at one of my free piano lessons, "Winter Scene."

Here we have a repeating pattern (ostinato) going on in the left hand while the right hand improvises a melody. Now, why is this such a great technique for beginners? Because most anyone can play an ostinato pattern right away! There is no note-reading, no theory, and **no requirement here other than being able to finger a chord.** And 99.9% of people can do this!

The first thing you notice with this lesson is the sound. It's a full rich sound that's created with the left hand. The ostinato pattern creates a harmonic background over which you can improvise your own melody. And it takes just a few minutes to do! You don't have to read music. You don't have to take years of lessons. No. You just have to learn a little about chords and you can sound like a pro faster than any adult student who decides to go the classical route and spend thousands of dollars on a piano teacher.

To learn and play piano fast, learn the ostinato technique. It can be used in many, many different musical styles and offers you a quick way to create your own music fast!

Learn How to Use Chords

L et's assume you've learned a few chords. Now what? What are you going to do with your new chords? You are going to use them to create music with and the best way to do that is to choose a key or mode to play in. This automatically limits your choices.

For example, let's say I sit down and start improvising and I start using a C Major 7 chord. I like what I hear but a problem arises - where do I go from here? This won't be a problem if you say to yourself, "OK. I started on C Major 7. Let's just stay in the Key of C Major and see what happens." Now, you are ready to go forward because you do not have a thousand and one confusing choices ahead of you. Do you see how this can free you up? You've limited yourself to using just six chords from the C Major scale.

Learning Piano Without Years of Lessons!

Y ou want to learn the piano. But you don't want to spend years learning how to read music.

That's understandable. Learning piano doesn't have to be the hard chore so many believe it to be. In fact, it can be quite easy IF YOU START BY LEARNING CHORDS!

For example, in the lesson, "Reflections in Water," we have four chords and a scale to create music with. We don't need to read music and we don't need piano tabs either. All we need is to learn how to finger one chord position and play the C Major scale. Then we can use these materials to create music with.

Learning piano this way is infinitely easier (and more rewarding!) than learning how to note read because we create it ourselves!

Once we have the chords under our fingers, we can explore the piano in a way that may never have been possible for you before. Many piano students don't believe they have talent or skill to improvise but this is simply not true. All that is required is the desire to try it. Once students jump in the water, they can't wait to take a swim and then they're hooked!

Learning piano without years of lessons is not difficult. All it takes is the ability to learn a few chords and then experiment with them.

Now, if learning classical repertoire is your goal, then of course you're going to have to learn how to read music. But reading music is not necessary in order to play the piano. Learning chords is!

Learning Piano by Listening to Other Pianists

When I first heard New Age pianist, George Winston play piano, I wondered to myself, "How does he do it?"

But it wasn't until I started creating my own music that the answers started to come. You see, if you've never played the piano before, it's almost impossible to understand what somebody else is doing on it.

After a while, I began to notice that the left hand played a much bigger part in creating Winston's sound than the right.

The reason I wanted to know all this in the first place is if I could figure out what he was doing, I could get the same sound myself. But that was only the beginning.

Soon, I could hear much more than chord changes and left hand patterns. I began to listen for the "form" of the piece... how the composer uses the tools of repetition and contrast.

In Winston's case, he will create a 4 or 8-bar phrase and loop it - improvising melody on top. This "method" really intrigued me for it seemed like an easy way to quickly "get down" music on paper. And it is! Instead of focusing on melody as the forward momentum that propels interest and the composition along, Winston creates an aural background and then changes that to create contrast. A perfect example of this is his piece, "Rain," where a gentle background mood is first created. He then follows this with a thunderous section - all played with the left hand.

Now, another way composers compose is by leading with melody. Here the melodic idea takes center stage and I can think of no other person to learn from better than John Herberman. Listening to his music, you hear how he uses repetition and contrast.

The first 8-bars is a complete theme for many of his pieces. This is followed by a contrasting section of 8 or 4-bars followed by repetition of the first section again.

All of this can be heard when you listen to music. A good idea when listening to dissect a piece is to listen for certain things. For example, you may say to yourself, "I'm listening for the form" and then focus on how the pianist is using form to create the composition. Other questions to ask are "What sound is being used?" Major? Minor? Modal?

Soon, you'll be able to understand the materials your favorite artists are using and then use them yourself in your own unique way.

Learning the Piano and Playing the Piano

Many piano students spend much time learning how to play the piano. Years upon years of study time is devoted to perfecting technique, tone, dynamics, etc. All the while, many of these same students have never really played the piano. They have spent their time practicing in preparation for the moment when they can "perform" for others.

Wouldn't it be refreshing if instead of learning how to play other people's music, we could feel confident enough to create our own? Why is it so daunting a task for most of us? I think it's because we've been taught that only a very few gifted individuals are capable of producing music from scratch - whatever the genre. Rock, jazz, classical etc. Unfortunately, this belief is enough to stop most dead in their tracks and for those, whose spark of interest was lit in childhood, it soon turns cold and lifeless.

Now, playing the piano is entirely different than learning the piano. Here we are at home. Why? Because we are playing. So different an approach it is too! Children are allowed free-play and are even encouraged to do so. But as we grow up, we decide we must "make something worthy of performance." What a tragic error in thinking, yet one that pervades the music world!

The solution is to understand that we all have our own special music inside of us and each and every one of us has something wonderful to share with the world. This something comes through when we stop learning how and begin to play the piano truly for the first time.

New Age Piano Lessons Give You Instant Satisfaction on the Keyboard!

Have you ever seen someone playing piano without sheet music and wonder, "How are they doing that?"

It's like magic to the uninitiated. They think this person must have years and years of piano lessons under their belt. And while some pianists do have years of classical training it doesn't mean a thing!

That's right. In fact, taking classical piano lessons can actually hinder your ability to just sit down and freely improvise. No, what most improvising pianists know is how to use chords. Chords and knowledge of the scale the chords came from is all that is needed to make music at the piano.

Now, most of you have heard of triads. These are three note chords that sound something Mozart or Beethoven might have played for their children to get them interested in piano. There's absolutely nothing wrong with learning triads -except for one thing... they're boring!

Listen to this...

What if you could learn a chord position that would give you a modern sound right away AND allow you to use both of your hands. And what if this chord structure could provide you with rich, lush sounding chords? You'd probably want to learn this kind of chord type over triads right?

Yet thousands upon thousands of piano students begin

their studies with the age-old chord structure known as the triad. Now, thankfully, you don't have to start this way.

Here's the point. We have Jazz and contemporary styles that go beyond the triad and begin with something called seventh chords.

But how exactly do we play these? By using something called the Open Position Chord structure. Here we use both hands to finger a modern sounding seventh chord. And we use over two octaves of the keyboard as well. With this kind of chord, we can instantly begin creating our own music.

How easy is this? If I were to tell you that you could begin creating your own music within one hour, would you believe me? Probably not. But if I were to show you exactly how to do it... well, then, that's another matter altogether. Don't take my word for it. Just take my free lesson at quiescencemusic. com and see for yourself!

New Year's Resolutions - Play Piano!

You've promised yourself you'd get to it. You've told yourself that when the new year rolls around you'd take piano lessons. So why don't you?

So many make New Year's resolutions to play piano yet never even get to a piano teacher. Why?

You're not sure about your own talents and abilities. Well, the good news here is that you don't have to worry about that. Not if you learn a chord-based approach to piano playing.

Many piano teachers make note reading the most important part of a student's beginning curriculum. But note reading is not necessary to make music!

For example, the lesson, "Reflections in Water," (available quiescencemusic.com) shows you how to improvise and create your own music right away using just a few chords! Imagine sitting down at your piano and creating your own unique music. It's possible. And it's a lot more fun than recreating something written over 200 years ago.

You can play the piano. And it can be quite easy but please check out a chord-based approach first. You'll be amazed at what just a few chords under your fingers can accomplish.

The cool thing about learning chords first is that you can immediately get involved in the music making process. And isn't this what playing piano is all about in the first place? Making music?

Actually, creating your own music is easier than learning how to play what others have written. Why? Because you're starting from a different place - a place of inspiration and creativity. It's a different approach to be sure but one that you're going to enjoy.

So, why not resolve to learn a chord-based approach to piano playing this year. Your New Year's resolution doesn't have to fall to the wayside. Just begin and see for yourself how fun and easy it can be!

Online Piano Lessons - Are They For You?

When most of us think about taking piano lessons, the last thing we think about is turning on our computer. But now, thanks to the Internet, you can take piano lessons online and learn from an online instructor. Let's see how this might work.

First, you need a computer with speakers. Most computers today either come with speakers or have them built in. If you need them, they are relatively inexpensive and can be purchased at any electronics store. It's important that your online lessons include audio samples. These will help you immensely as you get to hear your online teacher perform the example for you.

Second, you want to be able to communicate with the instructor. You're going to have questions so make sure there is a message board or forum available for questions and comments. Also, make sure your instructor actually exists! There are some websites that say they provide feedback to students, but this just may be an interactive forum with no instructor present.

Third, make sure the lessons you take are easy to understand. Do you want to learn classical piano? Then make sure the lessons you'll be taking aren't over your head. Do you want to learn how to improvise? Take a look around and see if you can actually do it from the examples provided.

Taking online piano lessons is a good choice for you, if you like to work on your own and take your time. There's usually no pressure to perform or complete tasks, so you can relax and work at your own pace.

Painting with Sound

Whenever I go to a Borders bookstore here in San Diego, I make it a point to look at the art instruction books. I'm not a visual artist, but I've always enjoyed the step-by-step approach authors of the better books take to teach students how to create a finished painting.

You get to see it all demonstrated within two pages or so. Everything is explained and, while I may not understand it by just reading about it (you have to do it!), a complete finished painting was always the goal - a very attractive goal too - for someone wanting to learn how to paint!

You have something worth working for by doing this. I've always wondered why music instruction couldn't be more like this. If you could explain, in a step-by-step approach, how to complete a piece of music, then students would be able to sidestep the tiresome harmony and theory courses taught at college and university.

This is what I've tried to do with my online piano lessons and while there is nothing wrong with learning theory, it's not the end all be all that many piano teachers would like you to believe.

Instead, a step-by-step method, where students get the materials they need to create with right away (scale, chords, and technique) can be used with great success! Students are able to use these materials to create unique compositions and improvisations of their own!

Piano For Beginners - An Easy Way to Play!

Ah, the piano. So beautiful. So elegant and wistful. But you can't play it for the life of you. At least not yet.

Piano for beginners has always been a somewhat difficult path. Here's what I mean. The hopeful student looks for a local teacher and asks about styles, rates, etc. Then the first meeting approaches.

You see your teacher and wonder just exactly what you're going to learn. Most likely, you will be encouraged to play in a classical style.

This means learning how to read music. It also means spending years and years learning how to play the classics. A noble goal and one pursued by thousands every year.

But what if there were an easy way to begin your piano studies? There is. And it has everything to do with learning a chord-based approach first!

What's that you ask? Simple. Chords are used to make music on the piano. Once you learn how to finger a few chords, you can make music. And not just the music written centuries ago. You can actually create your very own unique music!

What a difference that is. No longer "tied to the page" so to speak, the student who learns how to play chords on the piano is light-years ahead of his note-reading counterpart. How? Because by learning how to play chords, you learn theory. Once you learn a little theory, there really is no end to what you can play on piano.

I'm a big fan of the New Age style. Here, you can actually play piano right away. And with both hands using chords! It's exciting because a complete beginner can place fingers to keys and begin the act of creative playing.

Improvisation - the art of spontaneous invention is also a possibility for the complete beginner. That's right! Piano for beginners does not have to be hard and monotonous. On the contrary, it can be quite liberating!

Piano Keys And How To Make Sense Of Them

To the uninitiated, the piano keyboard looks like a sea of black and white. So many keys!

The way most piano teachers handle this problem is to first show students where middle C is -and I agree this should be the first thing newbies learn. But after they learn this visual marker, it's time to really make the piano keyboard easy to see. How? By showing students how to form chords.

Sure, you could spend your time learning every single note on the piano. And you'd probably still be confused as to how to make music. But if you learn a chord-based approach first, you'll be able to see piano keys as chords instead of individual notes. And when this happens you'll no longer be confused.

What I have my students do is master something called the open position chord first. Using this chord gives you a unique perspective to keyboard harmony. Both hands are called into play as you play something called a seventh chord. Seventh chords are used by contemporary pianists to create a "modern" sound.

In my free lesson, "Reflections in Water," we use open

position chords in the key of C Major to create a calm, gentle ambience.

Four chords are used in total: C Major 7, A minor 7, F Major 7, and G 7. If you're unfamiliar with these chords don't worry! You can learn them in a matter of minutes and start making music just as fast. Not only that, but you'll be able to learn and understand how to make music on the piano in the key of C!

You see, all you really need to know to make music and understand the keyboard is to know what key you're playing in and the chords from that key.

The key of C is located on the white keys. It's the perfect place to start your understanding of keyboard harmony. Once you can play the C Major scale and form a few open position chords on the piano, you'll see the keyboard in a whole new light!

Piano Lesson Books - The Only One You'll Ever Need!

There are a lot of piano instruction books on the market. Books on note reading, chord playing, etc. But there's only one book that puts together chord charts and chord playing to get you improvising and creating your own music.

So, what book am I talking about? It's called "*New Age Piano Made Easy*" and with it, you'll be able to quickly play something called the open position chord and then use it to create your own music. But how is this possible?

Simple. The open position chord is a modern sounding

chord structure that uses both hands right away at the keyboard. And with it, you can play modern sounds immediately. But just having these chords under your fingers isn't enough. You need a framework - something that will enable you to improvise and compose. That framework is the chord chart. Something most piano lesson books don't teach you about.

A chord chart is a "navigation" tool that tells you when to play a chord and for how long. It also tells you when to change chords. Jazz players use them almost exclusively because it gives a very clear and easy way to "follow the changes."

For example, the book, "New Age Piano Made Easy," contains over 80 improvisation exercises. Each one is designed to get you doing one thing and that is to play chord changes without thinking about it. That is, the goal is to be in the moment with the music. Something many students wish they could do but can't for one reason or another. Most of this has to do with the belief that what's coming out of you isn't good enough. The other belief that stops many students is the one where they keep saying they need to know more before they take the plunge into improvisation.

Nothing could be further from the truth! All you need is a few chords under your eager fingers and a chart and you're off exploring new worlds of sound!

It's very exciting for many students to be able to do this. Many of them are used to the note reading approach only and literally have no clue how to just sit down and "be" at the piano. Most of this has to do with attitude and the belief that improvising is difficult. They've seen people sit down and play off the top of their heads and are amazed. But there's a method to the magic.

Piano Lessons Can Be Fun!

There are essentially two ways to learn piano - note reading or chords. For those who want to spend years learning how to play other people's music, note reading is the way to go.

For those who want to create their own special music, chord understanding is a must - and much easier to learn. It is far better to learn how to make music first than it is to read it on a piece of paper.

Imagine a writer forced to copy another novelist's work. Insane right? But that's essentially what people do when they recreate another composer's work. It is not a creative act but a re-creative one because while the pianist's interpretation may be artistic, it does not mean that he created something original.

I'm not saying that great composer's works should not be recreated for others listening pleasure. I am saying that it's a good idea to understand that there is quite a difference between Beethoven composing something and someone else playing it.

Having said that, the benefit of learning how to make music first is that you understand the underlying principle of the thing. For example, let's go back to our fiction writer. If he looks at another novelist's work and the structure of the work, then he is beginning to see how the thing is made. This is entirely different than what goes on in the classical music world where a performer can read music, but does not know the principles that go into it's making.

Learn piano the easy way first. Learn how to first improvise, and then compose your own music. This skill is invaluable even if you do read music because you begin to see how the thing is made and once you can see this, your appreciation of it will increase tenfold!

Piano Lessons For Beginners - A New Approach

I f you're interested in learning how to play the piano and you're a beginner listen up. What I'm about to share with you will have you playing the piano in no time at all.

First off, forget about note reading. Forget about sheet music and trying to play Bach or Beethoven. While all of these have their place in piano lessons for beginners, it's not what I'm going to teach you. I promised you a new approach and that's exactly what this article will deliver.

Take a look at my free piano lesson, "Reflections in Water," (available at quiescencemusic.com.) The first thing you probably will notice is the title followed by what this lesson will teach you to do -namely using open position chords in the Key of C major to create a calm, relaxed atmosphere.

Notice anything here? This piano lesson actually looks like an art lesson, doesn't it! It's completely different as it takes you step by step through the process of actually creating your own music.

After you notice the title and the description of the lesson, you may also notice a small paragraph of text to the left that reads "materials used." Again, like an art lesson, you see exactly what you'll be using to create with. At the beginning of most art lessons, the author introduces you to the materials and techniques you'll be using to complete a finished painting. That's exactly what I do with piano instruction.

And my students love it. **It gets them playing piano almost right away.** Plus, it allows them to create music with modern sounding chords instead of the usual boring triads.

Note reading is not required for this approach. Just a little knowledge of chords. For the lesson "Reflections in Water," you'll see 4 chords and the keyboard diagrams they are laid out on. Once you get the feel for the open position chord, you'll love it and want to play the piano with enthusiasm. Why? Because it's fun! And it's easy.

And if that wasn't enough to get you motivated, there are also audio samples that let you hear how another pianist plays it.

Piano lessons for beginners do not have to be the same old boring thing most of us have come to know. They can actually be fun AND creative!

Piano Lessons Outside the Box: A New Approach to Learning Piano

Usually, piano lessons consist of a teacher assigning a method book to students in an attempt to teach them how to play the music of the "masters."

The hopeful student learns to read music (in a year or two) and begins to play his first pieces.

For most, this is satisfactory. All they really want to to do is play classical music and entertain themselves and others. Nothing wrong with it at all.

But what if there was a way to play the piano that allowed you to express yourself creatively -just like painters do? There is a way. And it all has to do with a chord-based approach!

You see, **chords are to the pianist as what colors are to the visual artist.** The artist uses color, form, and technique to create with. The improvising and composing musician uses melody, rhythm, and harmony to create music with.

Yet, the sad truth of the matter is music students rarely learn this art. If they do, it's after they've mastered note reading and piano technique. The truly creative stuff doesn't appear until well after, in most cases.

Now, I don't know why this is. But one thing is for sure... it doesn't have to be that way!

For example, by using a few chords and a way to play these chords, you can create your own music. Be it improvised or composed. Take my free lesson, "Reflections in Water," for example. We have four chords in the key of C Major. The chords are modern sounding seventh chords and are all played in open position. By using the materials of music (chords) we can quickly begin creating music - much like visual artists do.

You don't have to be Beethoven or Mozart to do this. On the contrary, the less you know, the better you will be able to improvise because you haven't learned what you "should" be doing.

I believe **piano lessons can be taught much like an art lesson.** You first have the title of the piece you'll be creating. You then use a step by step method that shows you how the piece was made. I've been using this method to teach with for years now and my students love it.

In short, don't think going the classical route is the only way. It's not. If you want to create your own unique music, you can!

Piano Lessons and Perfectionism

Are you a perfectionist? Does every note have to sound right before it comes out of your piano? If so, you might be cheating yourself out of the joy of music making. Most of us learned how to be perfectionists as children, trying to please Mommy or Daddy. We wanted their approval so we tried to get it right.

In the process, we learned that getting it right meant giving up happiness. It wasn't enough that we could express ourselves musically. We had to do a good job of it as well. As good as we could make it. Getting all the notes right. Trying to please music teachers who could care less if we were enjoying ourselves. All for what? To get a grade or a "that's good?"

It's a shame but this happens all the time in music schools. It's not until we become adults that we realize the damage that has been done. By then, it's usually too late and most never pick up an instrument again. What a pity that is. What a shame that we all must create to someone's standard of what good is. And worst of all, when you finally achieve that high standard, you are told that it is never good enough anyway.

The way out of this perfectionist's rut is to let go of the need to please others and refocus on pleasing ourselves. Now there is room to make mistakes and explore what art really is - namely EXPLORATION OF THE UNKNOWN! Here is where the real adventure begins, my friends. Here is where excitement truly is! Not knowing what is going to happen next. Not judging what comes out of us but being beholders of it all.

Improvisation is the key that unlocks this door. It is the one art form that is invention from one moment to the next. Experience the joy of improvisation and all need to get things right disappears. Just for a moment you feel like the music is playing you. Isn't that enough?

Piano Lessons for Seniors - Now Online

Used to be if you wanted to take piano lessons, you'd turn to your yellow pages and let your fingers do the walking.

Today, you can still let your fingers do the walking ... but online!

Piano lessons for seniors are here and are online. Some are free, some paid. But there are options available to those who want to learn how to play the piano.

The first thing you want to do is identify what you want to learn. Do you like the New Age piano style? Then I humbly suggest my site (quiescencemusic.com) Do you want to learn jazz or classical? These too are online and are actually free.

Many seniors are actively getting involved in the online world. And as more and more do, the need to cater to this demographic group will become greater.

Here are some tips you should look for when selecting piano lessons online:

How are the lessons organized?

Many piano lessons online are formatted as a PDF file or e-book. There's nothing wrong with this at all. In fact, it's just an electronic book. This idea is used quite a lot in the online piano lesson world.

Then you have actual lessons online with video and audio samples. If you're like me, you want to hear AND see what's going on. Now, with video being easy to implement and download, you can watch your piano instructor actually give a lesson online.

And last but not least, you have something where you're actually "live" with an instructor via webcam. While this option may intrigue some, it might not be the best use of your dollar as this type of instruction does cost money.

My recommendation? Look for lessons that have an instructor who uses video and audio samples. You can learn at your own rate and you won't feel rushed to "complete" assignments.

Piano Right From the Start: "Learning to Play What You Feel!"

Imagine being able to sit down at your piano, place your hands on the keyboard, and just play! Many piano students think the ability to do this requires years of study. They couldn't be more wrong!

Learning to play what you feel does not require extensive knowledge of harmony or theory. All that is required is the ability to do two things:

Believe that you know enough
Believe that you're good enough

Thousands of classically trained pianists are able to play Rachmaninoff and Bach but are unable to express themselves poetically at the keyboard. Why? Because of the above two beliefs! It's not enough to have mastered piano technique.

For example, many would be writers understand how to construct a compelling plot and know how a story should be written, but until they have freed their inner voice from criticism...until they believe that they are good enough to write that story, it simply won't get done!

The same goes for music and any other art. I can't tell

you how many times I repeated the above two statements to myself because I really wanted to get past my fear of being able to create music at the piano. I wanted to play what I felt at any given time - to be able to improvise. But this was nearly impossible as long as there was some voice in me that said I just wasn't good enough. And believe me, we ALL have these voices somewhere in our heads at one time or another.

Eventually, I got past the need to seek other's approval and realized that I was more important than the music. I learned that I already knew more than enough to play the piano. I also came to believe I was good enough and that no one person will every know it all or be a "perfect" player.

Piano Teachers - What's Wrong with Them?

Most of us like to use what we learn right away. So why is it that most piano teachers tell you can't really play music until you learn two years of theory or more? What hogwash!

If I had to wait that long before I could launch into my own creations I would go nuts.

Even art schools encourage creativity among their students. Certainly, a watercolor instructor would never expect her students to wait two years before creating a painting.

The same thing applies to writers. When someone wants to learn how to write a short story, the art and craft of storytelling is taught, sure. But does a writing instructor really expect his students to wait two years before plunging into the writing act?

Do you see where I'm going here? Music, especially classical music studies, have been stifling for way too long. Why can't music students enjoy the same level of creative freedom as visual artists or writers?

I've asked myself these questions and then tried to create piano lessons where a complete beginner could create his or her own music right away. And it worked! I now have students all over the world who tell me that this is the best method they have ever used to play piano with.

Please don't spend years learning theory you probably will never use anyway. And don't spend too much time with a piano teacher who really doesn't want you to play piano.

Piano Teachers And How To Choose One That's Right For You

How do you choose the right piano teacher? That's a question newbies at piano frequently ask. And it's an important question as well. Let me tell you how to do it.

First, you really have to **identify what your goals are.** Do you want to play classical piano pieces? If so, you'll need someone who's been trained to play this style. Fortunately, the classical style of piano playing has no shortage of piano teachers.

Do you want to play from fake books? If so, you'll need to find a teacher who knows chords. These teachers exist and can be found as well. While not as abundant as the note reading classical teacher, the chord-based approach is being taught more and more these days.

The first thing you should do is **check out your local yellow pages.** Turn to "piano teachers" or "piano instruction" and you should see more than a few listings.

Look and then call the piano teachers on the ads that you think may work for you. When you get them on the phone, ask them if they work with adults, children or both. If both, and you're an adult, ask them how much experience they have working with adults. They should have at least five years under their belt to begin working with you.

Also ask if they'll give you a free introductory lesson. Most will do this for you but be prepared if the answer is no.

As far as rates go, if you have to pay a little more for a quality teacher, do it. Like any other profession, there will be those who charge more who are actually worth it and those who charge more who aren't. That's why a free introductory lesson is a good idea.

Now, many **piano teachers are using the computer and Internet to teach.** The same rules apply here. See if they offer an introductory lesson. Find out how long they've been teaching and to whom.

Learning online is great if you're an independent person and do not need a teacher hanging over your shoulder. Also, online piano lessons are usually far less expensive and give you the ability to learn at your own pace; a quality many adults really appreciate.

Piano Tutors and
Why You Might Need One

Not everyone can learn piano on their own. Some people can, but they're rare. If you're thinking of learning the piano, you may want to consider getting either a teacher or a piano tutor.

What's the difference? Not much. It all really depends on what you need. Piano teachers usually take students by the hand from note reading to actual performance. A piano tutor, on the other hand, usually takes on adult students and helps them with specific problems.

These problems could be anything from note reading to how to play a particular passage on the piano.

If you're the kind of person who can tackle things on their own, a piano tutor may be the way to go. This way, you don't have to spend an arm and a leg seeing a teacher every week or 2 weeks. With piano tutors, you simply call them up on the phone and explain your problem or have a quick visit. Or, you can take advantage of modern technology and actually ask for help online.

The great thing about getting tutored online is that you can go back and forth with email. Most questions can be answered this way. If you're the kind of person who needs to be shown every little detail and nuance on the keyboard, this may not be the way to go. But if you're the kind of person who can take direction well, an online piano tutor will definitely save you time and money.

For instance, let's say you are working on a lesson and a problem arises. This problem could be one of interpretation or simply how to play a certain dynamic. If the tutor you're working with has the same material, you can tell him or her exactly what you're having problems with. And, if you have an electronic keyboard, you can actually record your playing and send it via email.

There aren't too many piano tutors available either online or off. Mostly, these people consider themselves consultants and charge a lot of money for their advice and opinions. There are places however where you can get all the help you need along with the piano lessons themselves. A Google search may be the best way to accomplish this.

Piano on the Right Side of the Brain

Some of you may remember a book titled *"Drawing on the Right Side of the Brain"* by Betty Edwards.

In this book, Betty Edwards tried to teach you how to see differently. She reasoned that once you could look at something with the eyes of an artist, you would be able to create like an artist. A simple idea, yet one that has helped many draw.

I wondered how this might also apply to music. Music is, at it's best, a right-brain activity. That is, the thinking left hemisphere is dormant while the intuitive right side is engaged in creative processes.

So how then can we play piano on the right side of the brain? The answer has to do with trusting ourselves. Once we sit down to play, we must allow ourselves the freedom to play ANYTHING that comes to the fore. If that anything is doodling and making nonsense noises, then that is what we must do.

Once we allow ourselves the freedom to play anything, we are sending a message to the creative right hemisphere. We are saying, OK, I'm giving in to whatever. I'll just play what I want. Now, once you can do this, PLAYING AROUND WITH CHORDS BECOMES AN EASY MATTER because you have given yourself permission to mess up.

Play Keyboards Instantly With This Easy To Use Chord Technique!

The first thing most students think they have to learn when playing keyboards is note reading. But not only is note reading unnecessary...it's a hindrance when you really want to play piano like a pro. Why? Because pros use chords. And chords are much, much easier to learn than reading sheet music.

While chords will help you play like a pro fast, it all depends on the kind of chords you play. For example, most fledgling piano students think they will begin by playing triads. And for most piano teachers, this is the chord structure taught at the beginning. While there is nothing at all wrong with triads (all western music is built on this) it just won't give you a modern sound.

A chord structure I have my beginning students learn first, the open position piano chord, uses both hands right away to create a modern sound!

The benefit of using both hands right away is that you can

vary the tones between hands to create a rich, beautiful sound that can NEVER be accomplished with the simple triad. Why piano teachers have their students learn triads first, I'll never know. But when you learn this chord position first, it allows you to create a open vented sound that is perfect for today's contemporary styles. Jazz, New Age, etc.. These styles can be created easily using the open position piano chord.

The way to play these chords is relatively easy. It may take a few minutes for your hands to get used to because this chord structure really stretches your hands. Here's how it works. The left hand gets the root note, the fifth, and the seventh. The right hand gets to play the third, seventh, and third again. So, if we were to play a C Major 7 chord, it would be spelled like this: LH -c, g, b RH -e, b, e. This looks a lot more complicated than it actually is and when you see it laid out for you on a keyboard diagram, you'll immediately see how easy it actually is to play!

To play the piano like a pro, don't start with triads; try the open position piano chord!

Play Piano Instantly -Even If You Don't Know Where Middle C Is!

You've been dying to play the piano. But you don't want to spend years learning how to read music. Of course you don't! And you won't have to IF you learn a chord-based approach to playing the piano.

Here's a method I use to get my students playing piano

in a flash. First, you need to learn a few chords. But not just any chord type. No. The chord type I have my students learn first is something called the open position chord. And with it, you'll be able to create your own unique music right away!

The open position chord is exactly what its name implies. It's a chord structure that covers more than two octaves of the keyboard AND uses both hands right away. If you don't know what an octave is, not to worry. Suffice it to say that two octaves are over 16 white keys. It's a handful to play this chord structure but once you master it, you'll be well on your way to unlocking the secrets of keyboard harmony.

So, how exactly can we use this chord to create music with? Easy. Take a look at my free piano lesson, "Reflections in Water" (available at quiescencemusic.com). The first thing you notice about this lesson is that it's unusual. It's not your typical piano lesson by far. In fact, you might even think it looks like an art lesson - and you'd be right! I specifically designed the lessons using a step by step approach that many art instruction books use.

The lesson contains four open position piano chords with fingering diagrams. The beautiful thing about this chord structure is that once you master it, you can easily use it to play ALL the chords in all 12 keys. The first thing I ask you to do is play the chords -first all tones together (solid chords) and then with the tones broken up (broken chords.)

Once you have this chord structure under your fingers and you've developed a muscle memory for it, the rest is easy!

In the lesson, "Reflections in Water," we use this chord structure to improvise a few minutes of music. The chord progression is laid out for you and all you have to do is simply follow along. I also provide audio examples so you can hear how I used the same chords to improvise with.

If you really want to play piano in a flash and don't want

to wait, try the open position piano chord. You won't be disappointed!

Playing Piano - A Whole New Approach!

Who doesn't want to play the piano? At one time or another, most of us have secret wishes of sitting down at a beautiful instrument and creating music. Playing piano is a joy. But most students aren't getting all they can out of their lessons. Normally well meaning teachers may be stifling student creativity by placing note reading at the forefront of the curriculum.

But what if there were a new approach to playing piano? What if you could just walk over to your piano or keyboard, sit down, and just start playing? Sound unbelievable? It isn't.

You see, the piano is a chord-based instrument. When you learn to play chords on the piano right away... instead of learning note-reading first, you learn how to really speak the language of music.

But not just any chord. What I have my students learn first is something called the open position piano chord. This chord structure allows the beginning (and more advanced student) immediate inroads into piano playing satisfaction.

This new approach allows you to play a modern sounding seventh chord with both hands right away! Compare that to the classical curriculum and there really is no comparison. Classical teachers begin with note reading and then take the quantum leap of having students learn triads.

Not that there's anything wrong with triads. They've been around for centuries and still deserve a place in the lesson plan. But most adults don't want to spend weeks or months learning triads. They want to be able to make music right away.

Actually, by learning how to play the open position piano chord, you can start creating your OWN music. The lesson, "Reflections in Water," (available at quiescencemusic.com) shows you exactly how to do just that!

Private Piano Lessons - Are They a Waste of Time?

Let me say from the start that I have nothing against private piano lessons. I think there are good teachers out there who can help you reach your goals. Having said that, I do have some things to say about them from personal experience.

My goal was to find a private piano teacher who could help me create my own music in the style I enjoyed - New Age piano. I knew a few chords, but what I really wanted was a mentor; someone who could already compose and improvise and help me do the same. And so I searched my city of San Diego for a teacher.

I found someone who I thought could help me (because of the brochure he mailed) and made an appointment. The first thing he did was assess what I already knew...which was what he was supposed to do. Fine. I showed him the chords I could play.

Then, for some bizarre reason, he started writing out chords on a piece of paper and that was the rest of the lesson! Talk about disappointing! And a waste of time and money.

I soon discovered, much to my dismay, that I probably wasn't going to find private piano lessons that would help me reach my goal. Now, if my goal was learning classical piano, there are literally thousands of teachers out there who could just whip out a folio and have me go through the book.

But I really wanted to be able to create my OWN music. Why was that so difficult?

My search finally took me to my local libraries where I discovered the books and materials to help me.

I'm not saying that there aren't any good private piano lessons out there. I'm saying there are other ways to reach your music goals.

Self-Expression Without Criticism

When I was nine years old I played the saxophone and thought I was pretty good at it. Unfortunately, I had a teacher who didn't think so and he went out of his way to make sure I knew how he felt.

One day, my mother bought me a new saxophone (it wasn't exactly new, it was used) but to me, it was the best gift I ever received. Now, of course, I wanted my teacher's approval and so I showed him my new instrument.

He called it a piece of s---!

Then the tears started to flow and from that moment on, I lost all interest in playing the saxophone.

Now, mind you, I loved this instrument. I loved the honking sound it made and the way it looked. I thought it was the coolest thing on planet Earth. But, getting that kind of criticism at such a young age destroyed my spirit and I soon found myself growing very disinterested in playing the sax.

Self-expression is a very personal thing. It's a thing that brings joy and happiness and can die very quickly if it is not protected and guarded from criticism. Even though I was a child and fragile, it is the child part of us that can become wounded if we allow others to walk over us - consciously or unconsciously.

Stop Playing Piano the Hard Way!

Let's face it. Learning isn't usually fun. It's a big drag. Especially when it comes to learning a musical instrument. Scales, repetition, and monotonous exercises abound. Most people love the piano but won't go near it for fear of not being able to play it. And most times, their fear is justified!

A typical beginning piano student scenario may go like this: You walk into the teacher's studio. He or she asks you what you want to learn. You respond with any number of choices; classical, jazz, new age. Then out pop the books. You know the one's I'm talking about. Hanon scales, Czerny. Maybe if you're lucky, you'll get introduced to a chord-based method. Maybe. But probably not.

You see, most piano teachers have this idea that you must learn how to read music before you can play music. That's nonsense!

In fact, it really works the other way around. You should be able to make music with chords and improvise first. Why? Because music is what the end result is. Music is not notes on a sheet of paper. It's hammers striking strings produced when a pianist fingers a chord. Children speak their native language first before they learn how to spell and write it. They have no difficulties doing this BECAUSE IT COMES NATURALLY! Music should be the same way! We learn the language of music by understanding how to use chords first. We then use these chords to create our music with.

There is nothing wrong with being able to read music, but if that's all you can do, you're limiting yourself creatively. Stop playing piano the hard way and learn how to use chords and improvise first. Because by learning how to improvise, you are actually speaking the language of music first!

Teach Yourself How To Play Piano Despite Years Of Lessons

You've taken piano lessons for years but you still can't play on your own.

You probably know the scales and can read sheet music, but you can't just sit down at the piano and make music.

Don't worry. It's not your fault. You see, literally thousands of people are just like you. They've taken piano lessons for years and while they can play a piece by Bach or Beethoven, they can't for the life of them figure out how to create something original. Something that is not written by a dead composer or that isn't on music sheets.

Here's the solution... Learn a chord-based approach to playing piano!

What's that you ask? Simple. A chord-based approach allows you to think and play like the composers you can play so well off of sheet music. Chords and the key they come from determine the sound of music.

You may think this approach takes a while to learn. Nope. Not at all. In fact, in my free lesson, "Reflections in Water," you learn how to play four chords right away - and you get to make your own music with them as well. In this lesson, you learn how to use open position chords in the key of C major along with broken chord technique to create a calm, reflective mood! And best of all - you can do it now... right away - without having any piano playing experience whatsoever!

How is this accomplished? Through the use of chords and the scale in the key of C major. You first learn the chords and the C major scale (which you probably already know) and begin to improvise with them. There are two audio tracks to this lesson that lets you hear exactly how it's done. Exciting? You bet. Difficult? Not at all. In fact, this may be the easiest, most fun lesson you'll ever get to play online!

The Case Against "Traditional" Piano Lessons

How would you like to spend four years in a university learning how to play other people's music? If you think this is ridiculous, you're right! Because that's what thousands of piano music students do each day.

They sit in front of their piano or keyboard with sheet music of a dead composer in front of them. Then they are told to "play it right." Have you ever heard of such nonsense? Imagine a budding writer forced to copy another novelist's work? In essence, this is what classical piano students do. They copy.

Although many think this is a creative act, it is not. It is a re-creative one. It's purpose? To give people who are told how to listen to music a chance to hear what is considered "good" music. Only in classical music is there such pomposity. And it exists because a very few people wish to hear the classics.

Let me tell you something. I love classical music. But I don't spend my time trying to recreate what has already been created. No. Instead, I want to connect with my own source and allow the music that is inside me to come out. I want to be creative too! And my philosophy is that anyone can be "a composer."

All it takes is the desire to create -to want to hear ones authentic self-expressed through music. Difficult? Not at all! It's as easy as putting fingers to keys and playing. Hard to believe, but true. You see, music students have been cheated from the get go by an academic snobbism that destroys the spirit and the will to create.

The suggestion is that the best music has already been created so why bother. The answer is crucial to our own well-being. We bother because it makes us feel good. That is all that is required and that is all that is needed to make music.

The Most Important Thing a Piano Teacher Can Give You

I've had a few piano teachers over the years. And I can't say that they really helped me. Why? Because I can learn technique pretty much on my own.

What I needed was for someone to help me TRUST MY OWN INTUITION and act as a mentor guiding me to my desired goal, which at that time, was to create my own music.

Think of a visual artist as an example. This artist may be able to understand and apply different techniques to create a pleasing work of art, but the art itself won't have that special "X factor" that only comes when an artist fully trusts their own intuition.

Intuition is the most confusing thing for someone without it to develop. That's because they've had a long time not trusting in themselves and their own unique talent and ability.

Nothing is more important for without the ability to trust yourself, you really won't be able to hear the intuitive voice that is always present and is always willing to guide you - if you let it.

The first step to accomplish this trust in yourself is to switch from a product oriented attitude to a process oriented one. You must let go of the need to produce something that is "good" or "bad." Instead, allow for mistakes and experimentation. Improvise and start out by using simple means. A few chords, a scale, some brief instruction are all that is required.

You must be able to play! Children trust themselves and their power of intuition without exception. They haven't learned how not to. I like to use the analogy of finger-painting as an example of this.

Put finger paints and paper in front of a child and watch what happens. They can't wait to get started in exploring this world of color and form. They're not concerned with good or bad. What they are concerned with is pure joy. And this comes from their ability to suspend judgment and just play!

Who Else Wants To Play New Age Piano?

O k. I know what you're thinking. New Age piano? You've got to be kidding me. Actually, I'm not. You see, I know many of you really love this style of music but are secretly ashamed to admit it.

I also know that somewhere in your CD collection, you have at least one New Age music disc floating around.

There's no need to be ashamed anymore. In fact, you can even learn how to play this style of music on the piano. And it won't take years, months, or even weeks to learn.

The truth is, you can begin learning how to play New Age piano music almost immediately. Here's how.

First, take a look at my free lesson, "Winter Scene." Here's a lesson that uses just two chords in the left hand. The chords are easy enough for most any beginner to master. Once the chords are down in the left hand, the right comes in to improvise an original melody from the D dorian scale.

This scale's notes are all located on the white keys to make it even easier for you. You simply get the pattern going with your left hand while your right happily improvises.

Now most people can't believe it can be this easy to begin creating their own music. But it is! The problem is many of you think it takes years of study to be "good" at the piano.

Fortunately, the New Age style of piano playing does not require you to be good. The only requirement is that you enjoy yourself at the piano. Something many adults would simply love to do!

Why Most Piano Teachers Can't Help You Create Your Own Music!

Most piano teachers have no problem teaching technique or note reading from textbooks. This is what they're good at. In fact, this is the bread and butter of their curriculum because they can make a lot more money by stretching out the "learning process" ad infiniti.

But, most piano teachers have trouble guiding students and helping them learn how to trust themselves. Why? Because they aren't trained in this! They're trained in getting you from point A to B and while this linear approach satisfies many... it won't help you with your own artistic expression.

If you want to spend years learning how to play other people's music (no matter how good it is) then great. You'll be taught this and you'll pay a lot of money for it. In fact, if you were to see a piano teacher every other week for three years or more, that's a couple thousand dollars right there!

And what will you have? The ability to read what other people have written in order to play what other people have composed. Think about this! Would any other artist, be it writing, painting, whatever.. spend three years learning how to write another person's book or paint another artist's picture? No way!

The bottom line is - if all you're interested in is note reading and playing other people's music, then most any piano teacher will do. If, however, you want to be able to improvise and create your own unique music, then find someone who will help you trust in your own unique talents and abilities.

Why Playing the Piano Can Be a Chore and What to Do About It

You're just not that into playing the piano lately? Not inspired? Feeling less than enthusiastic about putting fingers to keys?

I understand. I've been there and still experience what is commonly called "creative blocks." But you're not really blocked. You just don't want to play. Sounds weird, I know, but let me explain.

Art, any art is essentially a play activity. Let me ask you something. What happens when children are "forced" to play? They end up rebelling and doing exactly the opposite of what they were told to do.

Do you think you're any different? I'm always amazed at

teachers who suggest students bang their heads on the keyboard until they get it right. This is OK, I guess, if your goal is to become a concert pianist. But if your goal is to rise above the mundane realm of what I call "typist" piano, then you best get used to the idea that forcing never works.

Why is this? Because the artist part of you is really a child who just wants to play. Remember when you were young and you were in "the zone?" You didn't have to think about it. You didn't have to worry if it was good enough or if you knew enough. It could have been papier-mache, finger-painting, sprinkles...anything. The point is, your elementary school teacher understood that the process of play was far more important (and educational) than having you compete in an art contest to see who was better. The ironic part of all of this is that we ALWAYS discover more about our art when we do just play.

Life is hard enough already. Let's ease up on ourselves and actually enjoy the act of piano playing.

Why Playing the Piano by Ear Can Slow You Down Creatively

You've all heard the expression "play piano by ear" right? This refers to a musician's ability to pick out a tune, harmonize it, and figure out the rest of the song along the way.

A great skill to have no doubt. But, just having the ability to play by ear won't help you create your own music. Why? Because you still have to be able to improvise freely - a skill that is quite different than just picking out tunes on the piano.

Playing by ear assumes that you want to learn how to play other peoples music. Guitarists do this all the time. They'll sit around in front of the stereo strumming along to their favorite songs trying to figure out the chord changes.

Eventually they get it and can play these songs. Pretty impressive right?

But what if this same guitar player took these chords and relied on the heart instead of the ear to guide him? What if this guitarist decided not to try and imitate or copy what they "heard" on the radio and instead took those same chords and created something new and original? That's playing by heart!

It's very hard for most of us to trust our own intuitions. We're constantly being told we're not good enough, or not ready. By trusting your own intuitive mind first, you leap from way ahead of those who can only copy or imitate. You learn that there is another way of playing - a way where copying is not necessary and only serves to slow down creativity.

Look, there's nothing wrong with learning from those you love, but at some point, you're going to want to create something on your own. And unless you've exercised your intuition a little, you're going to have a hard time "coming up" with something. But, if we start out by trusting our own hearts and ourselves, we can quickly bypass this "copying" and launch directly into our own unique creations!

Why You Can't Play Piano

It's really not your fault. You've been taught that in order to play piano you need to first learn how to read music, and second, play other peoples music.

Don't feel bad. You're not alone. Thousand upon thousands of frustrated piano students long to understand the "mystery" of creating music on this fantastic instrument only to be let down.

They work so hard learning note reading that they miss the most important aspect - understanding how music works! Guitarists don't have this problem. They jump into chords right away and are satisfied immediately.

For some reason, chords are not emphasized when teachers set out to instruct students. Their agenda usually revolves around starting you out on a series of grade books that progressively moves you up until you can play other peoples music. Absurd!

Now, I'm not saying that note reading is a bad thing. I am saying that there is no reason to start studying the piano this way. If you start by playing chords, you will begin to understand theory. And you will join the ranks of creative people who get it. They know that melody and harmony make music. They get the harmony part first (chord understanding) and then the melody is easy to play!

Of course, there are other aspects of music making that a student must understand if he or she is interested in making music. But by starting with chords, the piano student has quite an advantage over their note reading counterparts.

Why You Still Can't Play the Piano

You've spent good money on books - workbooks, lesson books, other books on piano playing. But you still can't play the piano. Why not?

Two reasons. One, you lack motivation. That's understandable. After all, most lesson books require you to learn how to read music first then, play other people's music. Pretty uncreative, if you ask me.

Two, you haven't learned how to use chords. Music, real music is created with chords as the foundation. In music there are three aspects; rhythm, melody, and harmony. Harmony is created with chords. Chords can give you melody and rhythm. Weird huh? But once you have chords under your eager fingers, you're not far off from making music.

Now that you know chords are foundational for your creative success at the piano, you're left with what to play, or what style to play in. Most people just want to learn how to play the classics. They want to learn how to read music, so Bach, Beethoven and Mozart come to life through them. A noble goal but guess what? You're still playing other peoples music... no matter how good it is.

Wouldn't it be great if you could create your own music? But how you're wondering. Very easily by using chords! I'm a big fan of the New Age piano style. It's very impressionistic and attractive. Chords are used to create with and **a complete beginner can begin improvising AND composing music literally within minutes!** Fantastic sounds begin to appear and students are amazed what comes out of them.

Now they can truly play the piano. The creative juices flow as the warm sound of the piano floats in the air. Passersby wonder where that sound is coming from. You smile as they pass as your gift of music gently descends upon their ears.

Why a Guitar Player Can Teach You More About Piano Than a Piano Teacher

Do you know why more people want to learn guitar than piano? Because it's easier! And because students get to play something that actually sounds like music many times faster than their piano playing counterparts.

But did you also know that a guitar player can show you how to play piano better than most piano instructors? It's true! Here's why. <u>Guitar players use chords</u> and chord charts to create with. Piano players (for the most part) use note reading and memorization.

It's really easy for most beginning guitarists to quickly create music. In fact, you can learn three chords on the guitar in less than 15 minutes and start to play many, many tunes. Can piano players do that? Yes they can! But sadly, most don't.

You see, many people are intimidated by the piano. Not because of the instrument itself but because of the snobby stigma surrounding it.

The piano is held in such high esteem that people are actually afraid to go near it. Not the guitar. It's the everyman's instrument. Folk players, rock guitarists, and even Uncle Joe himself can pick up this instrument and soon strum out a tune.

A beginning piano player can also learn a few chords and just as easily create music as well as the guitarist. Now, the piano isn't often taught like this. Teachers can make a lot more money by stringing students along for years and years. With a chord-based approach, you can rapidly advance and learn how to play in most any style and it won't take you years either. How long will it take for you to learn a chord-based approach? Anywhere from one month to one year depending on how fast or slow you learn.

Here's the point. If you want to spend years learning how to play other peoples music, than note reading and memorization are for you. If you want to get creative and actually make music, look for teachers who embrace a chord-based approach to piano playing.

Performing

Common Thoughts That Kill Inspiration

Do you sit down at the piano and feel anxiety or peace? Are you anxious to begin creating or does the thought of being at your instrument bring you a sense of well-being? It all begins with what you're telling yourself. If you think that what you are doing is not good enough, it's sure to kill off that quiet little motor of inspiration.

The thought of not being good enough can put you into a deep freeze. It can stifle creativity and keep you stuck in doubt - a very nasty place to be in. Let's examine this thought of not good enough.

The first question that comes to mind is "not good enough for whom?" Who are you comparing yourself to? If you hold yourself up to someone, think about why that is. For example, I admire the playing of George Winston, but I'm not him and don't expect to be. His right hand technique is amazing and as much as I want to be able to play that succinctly, I just can't do it.

I accept that and really don't care so much about it. What's important to me is to be able to connect with my own creative source. This is the thought that keeps me grounded. If I begin to compare myself to another than I'm hopelessly lost and not focusing on what is truly important.

Another thought that kills inspiration is "I'm not ready." When will you be ready? Ten years from now? Next week? The fact is you don't need years of technical expertise to begin creating. If you wait another week or month or year to start, you will never begin and the world will miss out on your own unique voice. You are ready the moment you sit down to play. It all depends on what your goals are.

If your goal is to create a piece of music to perform for others, it will be ready after a certain amount of time. You, however, must be ready now. This means sitting down at the piano and being present in the moment. It all adds up bit by bit.

And last, but not least, is the thought that you don't know enough. Here's some news. You will never know everything and you will always be learning more. It never ends. I don't know everything there is to know about theory, chords, and harmony. Nobody does. But it doesn't stop me from experiencing the joy that comes from creating. This is your birthright and every creator's birthright.

Don't let the idea that you don't know enough stop you from creating your music. Even if you just learn what is in the free piano course, you know enough to begin composing, improvising and creating. Fortunately, in the new age style, you don't need to know sophisticated chord voicing or how to read music. You can jump right in and taste how sweet the act of creation is right away.

Piano Playing and Performance Anxiety

I'll never forget the first time I played the piano for an audience.

It was my first concert and it was fairly full up. I was to play my first CD, "La Jolla Suite," containing 12 pieces. There was to be one intermission and the whole concert lasted about 80-90 minutes.

Let me tell you that I was very nervous. So nervous I didn't think I was going to make it through. Suffice it to say that I really didn't enjoy myself. After many hours of trying to figure out why I was so nervous, the answer came to me - it was because I was self-conscious.

I was worried about how I looked, what the music sounded like, etc. I couldn't relax because I was too concerned about what the audience was thinking about me. And to this day, giving concerts is not my favorite thing. I realized that I didn't like being the center of attention.

What to do? For most people, myself included, playing in public is a fearful experience. Many suggest that you keep at it and eventually the fear will dissipate. But I ask myself why do it in the first place if you are scared. I have no hard and fast answers like many of the public speaking books would have you believe work. The truth of the matter is that some people are more comfortable in front of others. But one thing I think works is this: Start playing for very small groups of people and work your way up.

This desensitization process works better than most other methods because you learn that the audience is just made up of a large group comprised of smaller groups. If you can play for just one or two people and feel good about it, you are solidifying this experience. Then as you gradually play for more and more people, there is no fear because you do not carry it with you.

You see, if you play first for a large group, of course you will be self-conscious. But, by gradually building up, you don't create a situation where fear is generated in the beginning. Consequently, you don't carry it with you into larger performance spaces.

Sharing Your Music With Others

Y ou've got a few New Age piano pieces under your belt and you want to share your music with others. Can you do it? Yes! Here's a working plan for you.

Create 3 Pieces of Music

For those of you who are just beginning to improvise, don't worry about this. But for those who are beginning to compose, you'll need to have 3 complete pieces to play. Why? Because this will come to around 10-15 minutes of music - the perfect amount of time for a mini-concert! If you're in the process of creating your 3 pieces and haven't finished yet set a goal date. For example, it's a good idea to write something like this down:

By August 12, 2012, I will have 3 complete and polished pieces of music to play for others.

This is a time-based goal and will work wonders if you write it out and place it where you can read it everyday. Most likely, you will try and find excuses for why you can't finish something on time. This goal with time and date on it will continually remind you to stay on track.

Practice Your 3 Pieces

Practice is the only way you will build up your confidence level. Practice each piece slowly at first. Never back up if you make a mistake. I repeat... NEVER back up if you make a mistake. Why? What are you going to do when you're playing for an audience and you mess up. You're not going to stop everything and go back. No! You go forward. Chances are very good that the audience won't even notice. I can testify to this from personal experience.

When you practice, be with the music. The audience isn't really concerned with you per se. They want an emotional experience through the music and the best way to give that to them is for you to be in the moment.

Overcome Performance Anxiety

To do this, you must first practice until you can play all 3 pieces straight through and you must first perform for a very small audience. Perhaps one or two people. You see you have to get used to the idea that eyes will be watching you. This makes most very self-conscious. By playing for very small groups of people, or even one person first, you get used to this and you can simply shrug it off. Playing for others should be a joyful experience. It can be if you follow these simple guidelines.

Simple Piano Playing Tip Lets You Breathe New Life Into Your Music

What I'm about to share with you took me years to learn! And I'm still learning it. What am I talking about? I'm talking about something that will revolutionize your playing. I'm talking about being present at the piano while you're playing!

See. I told you it was simple. It's simple to say, but not so simple to do.

Let me tell you how I approach this. Some time ago, I sat down at my piano to work on some pieces for a new CD project. I'd completed the first sections on many of these pieces but the rest of the music just wouldn't come.

I can't begin to tell you how frustrating this was (and sometimes still is) for me!

Anyway, I decided to take a walk and figure out what the problem was. I started walking and unwinding and then it hit me... the reason nothing was coming was because of my own expectations. You see, I wanted to complete the pieces I'd been working on so badly that I was creating an atmosphere of anxiety. The joy of making music was gone. It was replaced for the need to create a product. And once this need appears, any progress is sure to be halted. Why?

Because the ego is never satisfied and wants something that is in direct opposition to artistic expression.

Now I have a different approach. I tell myself that my job is to just show up at the piano. To be present with the music. If new material comes, then fine. If not, that's OK too. Just as long as I show up and remain present to the process.

Tips on Performing Your Music for Others

Have you ever dreamed of performing a piece you created for others? And have imagined that they are captivated and held spellbound by the music? If you have, you know that it can be a long road from actually coming up with something, practicing it, to then giving it to an audience. In my own case, I had a good opportunity to perform. It was in a coffeehouse that already had a decent piano.

The problem was that I was playing for people who had come to listen mostly to guitarists on open mike night. Young guitarists that sang and played mostly Rock music or a derivative of it. I didn't care so much about that because I had the chance to go in front of people and share the gift of music.

In public speaking, it's said that the fear of standing in front of a group of people and talking is caused by the anticipation of losing face - of looking or appearing like a fool. Now, some may be able to get up in front of a group and actually feel better than they felt before getting in front of people, but the reality is that 99% of us are going to feel some kind of anxiety.

There are two schools about stage fright. One school believes that you can completely rid yourself of it (extremely hard to do and a somewhat unrealistic). The other says that you can never fully conquer the fear but you can manage it and reduce it to a level where you can function and perform.

So far, I'm in the second group and I've learned a few techniques that allow me to perform well. One is that I practice enough to where I feel confident that I can perform above the normal level. The second technique is to accept the feelings of fear and reframe it into the emotion of excitement. In other words, I may be scared, but I'm also feeling excited. I focus on that part.

Most of the performance anxiety will dissipate soon after your performance begins anyway. It's usually the first 10 minutes or so when you're the most anxious. My goal when I get on stage is to focus on and enjoy the process of sharing the music with others. My focus is not on the audience.

The best performances occur when you can completely forget about the fact there are people listening. Then they can share in the magic that comes through you.

Trusting Your Inner Voice - Key to Success at the Piano

We all have so many critical voices in our heads. They are telling us what's good, what's not, and what should be. We must stop the criticism if we are to play the music that is inside of us - but how? How do we turn off the inner critic and start to trust our inner voice? By listening to it. Most of us are taught not to trust our initial impulses, but it is this innocent prodding that brings authenticity in our improvisations and musings at the piano.

To deny these impulses is to deny yourself of what is truly rich and necessary for creating a music that is full of both joy and longing. Combine these two and you have the secret duality that is in the best music. It's something you can recognize immediately, yet it's hard to put your finger on exactly what causes it. It's a combination of sadness and joy. Cast everything aside. What you want is not important and will hinder your ability to hear the inner voice.

Whenever you want to create something, you set yourself up because you block that small inner voice that says, "Let me go where I will." Your ego may think it won't be happy with the results. Your ego wants people to say "Ah what a great job you're doing. You really can play well." These comments can set you up to think that you are really great. This is false gratification and, contrary to opinion, not healthy self-esteem.

Puff yourself up all you want, but **if you want to really feel the connection between yourself and the music, you will have to abandon what you want and, instead, let your inner voice decide.** It may not be the kind of music that will get you on American Idol. It will be the kind of music that will get you to a special place few can know - that place where you disappear and the music appears out of thin air. The feeling you will get from this will far surpass any kind of ego gratification that may come from fame or fortune.

Style

An Easy Way to Get the New Age Sound

When I first stumbled upon the Open Position Chord, I knew I had discovered something special! Here was a chord that had its notes spread out over two octaves! With this much space, the sound that is produced is beautiful and wide open - hence the name of the chord. And it's perfect for the New Age style of piano playing! For example, in lesson 26, "Rabbit in Snow," we use the OPC to create with. The chords are chosen. The key is set in A Major. Now all that is left to do is improvise.

With this set of limitations, it becomes a matter of playing around with the possibilities. I use the chords and the element of time to create. My left hand usually stays in the initial position while my right is free to play melody. It leaves the initial position but always returns to the OPC configuration.

To use the OPC, one must be able to play with it without worrying too much about what's coming out. The more you "play," the more you will discover. Not by trying or forcing, but by allowing. The secret to using this chord position is to play around with its innumerable possibilities. Here is a chord structure that allows you to play with both hands right away, and is perfect for the New Age style!

Arranging for New Age Piano

A while back, I wrote an article that compared flower arranging to music arranging. While this may seem a world apart, it really isn't.

In flower arranging, the goal is to create a pleasing whole using different flowers, colors and textures. If you've ever seen a beautiful flower arrangement, you'll know what I mean. The eye takes in the various contrasts and colors and is pleased when it forms into one satisfying whole.

In music the object is the same. When arranging a piece for New Age piano, we work with sections. We can label the sections "A" and "B" and then "arrange" the sections into an order. The most common order is ABA form. It has the benefits of simplicity and is a good place to start with New Age piano.

Most times, I'll use an 8-bar phrase for the "A" section. This gets repeated two or three times. Then it's time for some contrast - the "B" section. This can be a 4 or 8-bar phrase depending on taste. Then the "A" section is repeated one last time.

There are other elements that go into our arrangement such as introductions, transitions, and endings. Using these elements, we can create a pleasing musical arrangement that satisfies the mind's need for order and beauty - creating art!

Bob Ross -
Art Teacher Extraordinaire!

For those of you who don't know, Bob Ross was a painter who specialized in showing people how to paint complete landscape scenes in about a half-hour. I've never really painted before, but I've always loved watching this man paint on TV. He hosted a PBS series for many years.

The thing about him that inspires me is his attitude. I'm sure he knows that he's not creating "masterpieces," but he doesn't seem to care. In fact, just watching his happy, serene face for 30 minutes proves my point about creating. His focus is on enjoying the process. And art is a very subjective thing anyway.

Bob has many critics who "accuse" him of skirting technique in favor of quick and easy sketch pieces. But this kind of criticism is inane because what is produced is art that produces emotional responses.

Since when does a landscape artist have to explain his methods to others? In fact, Bob Ross's technique is revolutionary for he showed you how to produce a work of art very quickly! If Monet or Manet could do this (and they probably could) then who's to say Bob was wrong for doing it?

Many people love his art. And those who don't are usually the "serious" artists who need constant validation from the outside world to prove their worth. Bob died in 1995 but his show still lives on.

Classical Piano Lessons - What to Do When You Finally Get Tired of Them

Ah ... classical music. Let me say from the outset that I love classical piano. Beethoven, Bach, and Mozart are all wonderful composers who have contributed much to the music world.

But what to do when you don't want to spend years learning how to note read?

Well, you could study jazz. This genre is a big believer in improvisation. And there's no denying this is far more "creative" than the note reading approach. Jazz pianists use chords and something called a lead sheet to create music.

But jazz requires much in the way of theory. Altered chords, polychords, and harmonic analysis play a big role in the jazz students curriculum.

And then there's New Age piano. There is no waiting and no need to get a lot of theory under your belt. Students can learn a few chords and jump right into their own unique creations.

While classical piano lessons make sense for those interested in performing the music of the "masters," it can be a big detriment to those who want to express themselves creatively with a musical language that is part of this century.

New Age piano uses modern chords and a modern sensibility to create a type of music that is now being created and recorded by today's composers. It's exciting to be a part of something that is happening now rather than something that happened a long time ago.

And the best part about this is, you can be a part of it. In fact, I've had students who were able to create their own music within a few weeks, not years. And it's all due to the way instruction is given.

Students are encouraged to be creative from the start. A few chords, a scale, and a way to play them is given. Then, students can plunge in and begin creating.

If you're looking for a quick and easy way to be more creative at the piano, I heartily recommend the New Age piano style.

Digital Pianos - Are They Right for You?

Many families are now purchasing digital pianos to learn on. And why not? They're relatively inexpensive, take up very little space, and produce high quality grand piano sound. But there are certain drawbacks to owning one.

For example, it's a good idea to play an acoustic instrument before trying a digital one. Why? Because no matter how well the piano sound is sampled, it will never match the pure acoustic sound and richness of a "live" piano. This factor is very important to some because they want to experience that organic sensibility only a true acoustic can give them.

When a key is struck on an acoustic instrument, it produces overtones that reverberate around the room creating a sound that no digital instrument can accurately capture. I don't know why this is but I've played on the best digital pianos and have never experienced that "woody" feel an acoustic gives out.

If this doesn't concern you, then you've passed the litmus test for owing a digital piano because while they can't give you the exact feel of an acoustic, they come pretty darn close to giving you the deep, rich, full sound of a grand piano! For most people, this is all that matters and I for one agree!

Today's' digital pianos are so good that most listeners can not tell the difference between a "live" piano and a digital one. Add to that the fact that they are the most affordable of the kinds of pianos you can buy and you've got an instrument that's hard to beat.

It really all depends on what your needs are. Do you need to experience a cacophony of overtones? If so, don't go digital, But if you want that full grand piano sound without paying $50,000 for it, digital is the way to go!

Empty and Marvelous

Empty and marvelous is a phrase from one of Zen practitioner and philosopher Allan Watts' books. It represents a state of being where desire is gone and only acceptance of the present is known.

In a way, that's what improvisation is about too! We empty ourselves of ego and allow the music to take us away. We are amazed by this process because it seems that the music has a life of its own - if we let it. This requires a certain attitude that many find hard to attain because of the need to be in charge.

If we learn to empty ourselves of what kind of music we

want to create, we come up with something that has a special quality that could never have been created by ego alone! This is the "X factor" that is missing from so much music today.

Here in the West, we are used to achieving something. We want a good music, a nice music, or something that is worthy of performance. We don't want music to change or transform us. This wouldn't be something we could use. We aren't used to attaching value to something unless it can do something for us. But it is exactly this kind of music that gives us so much and has much to offer!

If we play and enjoy the process, just for process's sake, we begin to understand the true meaning of the phrase "empty and marvelous." We begin to feel the music and know that something special is taking place. It's like a musical meditation that heals and comforts, not just the player, but everyone around who is fortunate enough to be listening.

Five Secrets to Playing in the New Age Style

1. Learn how to improvise

Learning how to improvise is the key to playing in this style. Period. You must learn to experiment and take musical risks - within certain frameworks, of course. You're not going to bang on the keys and expect to make music. This is not the kind of risk I'm talking about. Students thrive best when given a certain set of rules or guidelines to move around with.

For example, in the lesson, "Reflections in Water," you are

given a few chords and a specific scale with which to make music. In other words, I give you a set of limits from which you play the game of improvisation. This will free you up from the thousand and one choices you could possibly have. In fact, if you didn't have a set of limitations, you probably would end up banging on the keyboard because while it is important to be free and spontaneous, it is equally important to understand how the game is played.

2. Develop the proper attitude

This one ties for first place. In my opinion, what stops most students from learning all they can from this style is the attitude that they either aren't good enough, or are not ready to learn how to improvise and play piano. Please don't think that. No one person will ever know all there is to know about any one subject let alone piano playing. You will always be growing but you must start somewhere and you must start from SIMPLE means.

Here's a quote that sums it up best: "In the beginners mind there are many possibilities, but in the experts mind there are few." This means that you have an advantage over so-called experienced piano players. Your attitude should always be one of receptivity. That is, never force anything to happen because when you force you are already setting your-self up for failure and disappointment.

3. Forget what you were taught

Perhaps you were taught that you must learn your scales first and that you must learn how to read music before you can do anything else. I'm here to tell you that I can't read music, yet somehow, I've been able to put out two CD's of original music! In fact, if anything, reading music will slow you down creatively! If you want to create your very own music, you must forget what you were taught about music in general and focus on learning how to improvise first and compose second. Both of which can be taught!

I think I read every book at the library on composition and improvisation and what helped me out the most was a very slim volume on chord changes using 8-bar patterns. By playing the chords in a set framework (8-bars) I was able to see how to use repetition and contrast to create with. And of course, I listened to the people I loved and learned a lot from just listening. So forget about what you were taught and start thinking about what you want to accomplish and you can do it!

4. Learn chords

You've heard it before. Learn chords and you can make music. Just learn the 144 chords and voila! You can do it all. Don't believe it! You need to learn chords, but you don't need to learn one hundred chords right away. No. You need to learn probably about 3 chords or less to begin improvising in the "New Age" style. And if you think that you need to learn more than this at the beginning, you are wrong.

Of course, you can learn as many chords as you want but what's the point if you never use them? It's like learning a new vocabulary word each day for the sake of massaging your ego. Nice, but unnecessary.

5. Learn how to use Chords

Let's assume you've learned a few chords. Now what? What are you going to do with your new chords? You are going to use them to create music with and the best way to do that is to choose a key or mode to play in. This automatically limits your choices.

For example, let's say I sit down and start improvising and I start using a C Major 7 chord. I like what I hear but a problem arises - where do I go from here. Now this won't be a problem if you say to yourself. "OK. I started on C Major 7. Let's just stay in the Key of C Major and see what happens." Now, you are ready to go forward because you do not have a thousand and one confusing choices ahead of you. Do you see how this can free you up? You've limited yourself to using just 6 chords from the C Major scale.

George Winston and New Age Piano Playing

The first time I heard George Winston play back in the early 1980's I was blown away. I didn't know why I liked this music. All I knew was that it made me feel good and that was enough. I didn't even play piano back then but something about this music seeped into me, almost haunting me. The way he let the notes ring out and wasn't concerned with pop flavorings. It was a new sound for the time.

When I began to play piano, I wanted to know how he did it. How did he create this music? I read somewhere that his method was to create the chords first, then improvise a melody over them. Great, but what chords and how do you know where and when to play them?

I then realized that George wasn't really doing anything radically different than most classical composers who think in sections. Composing is all about using the techniques of repetition and contrast. In most of Winston's music, there is a lot of repetition going on with the contrast coming from the melody. The chords are repeated in certain patterns, the melody played on top, but there still is a framework operating here.

For example, if we take eight measures of music and call

it an "A" section, we have composed. We have taken chords, put them into some kind of order (no matter how tightly or loosely) and have composed. It takes a certain skill to keep the music fresh after a certain number of repetitions. This skill has to be practiced. It cannot be taught. This is a doing operation. You can listen to music, but to learn improvisation and composition, you must do it.

Now the secret is this: You may repeat a section as many times as your interest remains with the music. As soon as you become bored in your improvising, so will the listener. For most, having one section isn't enough therefore we bring in the "B" section. This could be anything from 4 to 8 bars of new material. This new material is also repeated and eventually we return to the "A" section. When you start to think in sections, you can unlock the mystery of most music.

Music Making as Spiritual Experience

If you've been playing piano for some time, you may come upon periods where you forget yourself and only the music remains. You might even have had a spiritual experience. A phenomenon where emotion and intellect become one and the outside world disappears.

This experience is what we all want, whether we admit it or not. This is a very important part of making music - especially new age music. We want that moment where we can stop thinking and start feeling.

Of course, there are times when we create something for a specific purpose such as dance music, rock and roll, etc. But, when you are attuned to your feeling and letting the music flow from your fingers, the wonder and magic of it is enough to make you want to come back again and again for more.

To get to this place does not require any special ability. It only requires that you know a little about chords and how to use them. Then, you place your fingers on a chord and off you go.

What makes this complicated for some is their indecision about which chord or notes to play. After all, there are thousands of choices. The solution for this problem is limiting your choices. In the free lessons, I give you a scale to play and a few chords from that scale to improvise with. This is enough material to get the imagination going. Some students thrive on limits while others fight them. I fought them too until I realized that my goal was to feel good about music making - not to create a masterpiece.

As soon as I thought about creating anything, I froze up. Technically, I knew a lot but it did me no good. I reexamined my reasons for making music and came to the conclusion to keep it simple. Simple, in my mind at the time, meant boring. But I finally let go of the need to please others and as soon as I did, I began to experience music making as a spiritual experience.

There is nothing that heals me so much as just being at the piano and letting the notes fall where they will within the limitations I set for myself. First, I allow myself to gravitate to any sound that calls me. For example, it could be a minor chord. It might be the pentatonic sound that calls to me. Then, I simply stay within that sound or tonality and all is well.

Music Therapy and New Age Piano

If there was one genre of music that's perfect for music therapy, it would have to be New Age piano! Soothing and relaxing, the piano offers many benefits to those in need of respite. The wonderful thing about this style of music is that it's also easy to learn how to play!

A few chords, a scale, and you're able to make music. And not just any kind of music, but one that's conducive to alleviating stress. Let's look at how one might go about learning how to play piano in the New Age style.

First, it's best if you learn one chord position that will give you a nice modern sound right away. The open position chord structure accomplishes this. It's easy to learn and can be used by the beginner right away to make music. And it uses both hands as well to cover more than two octaves of the piano keyboard!

Once this chord structure is practiced, it's time to add in a few chords. Just a few chords is all that is necessary for the beginning adult to experience the joy of improvisation. The hands are placed on the open position chord structure and the fingers move around creating melody. Nothing more is required than an openness to explore the possibilities.

And once students get started, they find that they can't stop playing. The therapeutic aspect of this comes from the free-form improvisations students are able to play only after a few minutes of practice. They begin to unwind, relax, and forget about the problems and cares of the day. It's a music therapy that goes one step above just listening to music.

Nature Sounds and New Age Piano

I f ever there were two things made for each other, it would have to be New Age piano music and nature sounds. After all, New Age piano gets much of its inspiration from the natural world. There are many CDs available that have this classic combination. Let's look at a few of them.

1. Forest Piano by John Herberman

This CD is in my opinion the best New Age piano CD one can buy. And it has nature sounds too! John Herberman is a very talented pianist/composer who's music seeps into your stressed out psyche and gently massages you. Each piece is a unique composition that is sometimes melodic, sometimes textural, but always beautiful. You'll wear your CD player out with this one.

2. Piano Cascades by John Herberman

OK. I'm a big fan of this man's music. I admit it. In fact, the minute I heard this CD in an "Images of Nature" store, I had to have it. So delicate and beautiful is this music that you'll think you're actually in the middle of a waterfall. The nature sounds, supplied by Dan Gibson, are first rate and do not overwhelm the music. In fact, both piano and nature sounds blend together into one magnificent whole creating a fresh ambiance that will revive and cleanse your spirit.

3. San Juan Suite by Michael Gettel

San Juan is an island off the coast of Oregon, where the mighty Orca whale is known to live. Michael gets his inspiration from the natural beauty of the area and, of course, this black and white whale. The music is superb with nature sounds interspersed here and there for effect. The music gets first dibs here with the nature sounds delicately placed in just the right places.

If you love nature and music, you will love these CDs. You can find them on major online CD retailers.

New Age Music - How It's Made

Different styles of music have different "sounds." We can all pretty much agree on that point. For example, jazz uses seventh chords almost exclusively. This, and the kind of chord progressions used in jazz, gives it its unique flavor. But what about new age music? Does it have it's own special ingredients? Yes it does.

Now, there are no hard and fast rules here but for the most part, new age music is a consonant music. That is, there is little or no harshness going on in the music. No saxes wailing and what not. Having said that we can eliminate most of the tense jazz chords and their voicing. So what are we left with? Mostly major and minor chords based on the regular scales and the modes. The chord progressions are simpler and usually start on the l chord. No ll-V-l progressions here.

What about melody?

In jazz, we have a soloist who usually plays a lot of chromatic notes. This is rare in new age music because it would create dissonance. New age melodies tend to be softer and more on the spiritual side. Solos, if there are any, are not so much concerned with the expression of the self than they are with letting the music express itself. A subtle but very important distinction. Jazz players may have some ego invested in their performance. New age musicians learn to let the music play them. They learn to become a channel for the music itself allowing it to speak through them. Of course, I'm not saying that this can't happen in jazz, but, just watch a jazz performer and you'll see what I mean.

Last but not least is rhythm.

Let's do a comparison/contrast between Jazz and New Age music. Jazz has a definite discernible rhythm. It is what makes Jazz jazz. New age music can have a pattern or an underlying rhythm to the music. It can be used to create trance like states in the listener. Drums are usually a part of jazz music. Percussion is mostly absent from the New Age sound simply because it would not add to the atmosphere most New Age musicians create. Timing is very important to the jazz musician. The soloist has the freedom to play whatever he wants as long as he maintains the meter and stays in time. New Age music is more elastic in that timing is there, but is not a master of the player. The New Age player can disregard time altogether. Just listen to Zen flute music as a good example of this.

Now, what does all this mean for the aspiring New Age musician? A couple of good things. It means that there is a definite "New Age sound" out there. That it is here to stay and that people like and need to hear it. And it means that there are some guidelines out there for what defines the meaning of New Age music.

New Age Music - What Is It Good For?

Let's face it. The world will not end if there isn't another new age music CD on the market. So why bother? Why play when most people don't care or want to hear the kind of music you like? The answer lies in the nature of art itself, for the world really does not need art. It can survive without painting, sculpture or music. It can survive, but it would be a pretty dreary place.

But the main reason we play is not for the world but for ourselves. We must play for ourselves first and if people hear and like it fine. If not, that's fine too, as long as we don't deprive ourselves of the enriching experience improvisation can bring.

When I first started playing, I wanted to create something others could admire. Something that people could say, wow, listen to that. That guy is really good. But I was miserable and miles away from the true purpose of playing music. It wasn't until a year or so later that I realized that if I don't please myself first, no one would be pleased. Nor did it matter if others were pleased or not.

So, what is New Age piano improvisation good for? Absolutely nothing - except the joy it can bring to you and to me when we enter the flow and the music pours out of us. It is so precious to be able to do this. So fleeting it may be too. A second or a minute of forgetting yourself at the piano is a sacred act. One that grows and develops. It matures of itself. Much like meditation. If one practices the art, one grows in proportion to that practice.

This kind of growth is spiral in nature. There are times that the music seems lifeless and dull. At these times, we feel the same inside. But a day or two later, we are in a new place and the music flows like water. This is a mystery, this process.

One can only go with it and not fight it. You are creating art second by second when you improvise. This kind of beauty is fleeting - but is the most precious. Guard it. Cherish it. And if you feel inclined, share it with the rest of the world.

New Age Piano: Capturing the Beauty of Nature

Landscape artists do it. So do nature photographers and wildlife artists. They capture the beauty of nature in their art. Now we have New Age piano. A beautiful style of piano playing that very gently guides the listener on a quiet journey into nature's wonders.

Using music to describe nature is nothing new. Composers have been doing it for centuries. But nothing really contemporary and accessible to the average listener has been produced until the "New Age" genre hit the scene in the early 1980's.

Led by pianist/composer George Winston, his album, "December," revolutionized piano playing and allowed millions of people to experience something with more substance than the average pop song. There was something about the music that immediately put you in a trance. Here was music where the spaces between the notes were as important as the notes themselves.

The "December" album cover featured a stark winter landscape and was very minimalist in design. This was done on purpose since the music itself is minimalist. Focus is not on sophisticated harmonies or fast melodic runs. Instead, unique atmospheres are created by the use of letting notes ring out. This was something that seemed a perfect match for nature itself. A relaxed ambient approach became a perfect marriage to nature's own quiet beauty.

On Winston's album, "Autumn," titles like "Road," "Moon," and "Woods" allowed listeners to journey into the composer's interpretation of these places. Thoughts of long walks in the woods or memory of a special place seemed to come up easily as you listened to the music. George Winston was a pioneer for the simple reason that he introduced a whole new genre of music to the listening public. He combined his two loves of music and nature into what has now become known as New Age piano.

New Age Piano Music - My Top Picks

When it comes to New Age piano music, I have a few favorites. In fact, there are really just 2 people that come to mind. And both of them have completely different styles. I'm speaking about George Winston and John Herberman.

George Winston literally put New Age piano music on the map. Of course, there were others before Winston who specialized in this genre (namely Steven Halpern) but it was Winston's album, "December," that skyrocketed this style of piano playing into popular culture.

To say that this music was and is different than what most people usually listen to is an understatement. And really, this kind of music shouldn't have been as popular as it was, but when this album came out in the early 1980's it captivated a large audience.

I think it may have to do with its accessibility. So many people are afraid of classical music because they think they have to "figure it out." It is, for the most part, much more organized and subtle than what most people listen to on a daily basis.

Then along comes Winston with "December." Here was music that sounded classical, yet wasn't. It was more atmospheric and easily digestible. In short, it gave listeners an experience of something profound. Yet it was easy on the ears.

My next favorite New Age pianist/composer is John Herberman. Most of you probably don't know who he is. He records for the "Solitudes" label. "Solitudes" combines nature sounds with music.

When I first heard Herberman's music, I was in an "Images of Nature" store in La Jolla CA. And I have to tell you that I was immediately spellbound. It literally put me in a trance. So poignant and beautiful were these simple melodies. And played with the hands of a master.

Herberman's style is very different than Winston's. A much lighter touch is employed, yet the music that comes out is sublime.

If you're into the New Age piano music genre, I highly suggest listening to "Forest Piano" by John Herberman and "December" or "Autumn" by George Winston. You won't regret it.

New Age Piano Music and Those Who Hate It

'll never forget the first time I read the joke... "What do you get when you play New Age music backwards?" The answer really cracked me up... "You get New Age music."

It's a point that's well taken. But the people who put down and criticize this style of music are really missing the point. You see, New Age music isn't about trying to create sophisticated sonatas or perfect preludes.

It's really about a feeling. A feeling that goes through you, allows you to relax, and perhaps take a breath from the hectic pace of life. It's about spirit... allowing the music to flow through you and transport you to a more peaceful place.

Still, there are those who insist this music is nothing but aural wallpaper - not to be taken seriously and to be put down at every chance.

Well, they have one part right. It's definitely not to be taken seriously. **It's to be enjoyed** - a concept that many "serious" musicians have a problem understanding. And this is really not their fault.

Academic snobbism in the music world does exist. It equates "good" music with "sophisticated" music. But not only is this a useless comparison, it's harmful as well.

The simple truth of the matter is, we like what we like. As soon as you try and instruct someone on why they should like something - whether it's because it's supposed to be good, or because it's considered to be a master work of art, danger sets in. Why?

Because once you lose trust in yourself, once you start to doubt what you really like, you'll start to lose an important part of yourself. That innocent trusting part that simply knows what you like and love and doesn't need someone to point it out.

Piano Class Very Unsatisfactory

'll never forget a piano course I took when I was attending the Community College of Philadelphia. It was a "class" piano course with about 20-25 people were seated around keyboards. Each keyboard had headphones and we were supplied with a standard piano textbook.

The course lasted four months or so and I learned how to play triads with both hands. I also learned how to read treble and bass clefs.

I can't say that I was thrilled with this course. In fact, I remember thinking how boring it was. And dry. Why couldn't we learn something that would allow creativity in?

I guess most "teachers" don't think you can be creative in music until you spend about two years learning what they consider to be the basics. This is all nonsense and only serves to mystify music and make it inaccessible to the masses.

I can only say that during the 16 weeks or so of attending this class, I learned that I didn't really want to play the piano. Why? Because I wasn't having fun! And fun is the impetus for further exploration. It seems like common sense to me. Yet this idea of actually enjoying the process of making music eludes music teachers at the college level.

Ironically, elementary school teachers know that their students MUST HAVE FUN first or they won't be interested in learning more. Children spend their time in musical activities that inspire imagination and create a sense of joy. How interesting that this same educational technique is not employed for the grown ups among us.

Of course I'm not saying that adults should spend their time skipping and hopping on musical notes to learn them. What I am saying is that it's important that joy and love of music be placed before theory and discipline.

Play Piano in the New Age Style

t's not what you play, it's how you play it. These words summarize the art of piano playing in general and New Age piano playing in particular. You could take two chords, and, if you were in the moment and in flow, communicate the utmost emotion and power.

However, give the same two chords to someone who is more concerned with image than music and the sound won't have the appeal - the attractive quality that pulls the listener closer like honey to a bee.

The secret is not how much you know or how good you think you can become. No. The secret to the art of New Age piano playing is being able to forget yourself and express yourself without ego. Then you will begin to understand the meaning of art. For it is only when we transcend ourselves does something real appear.

What comes out of you is something from you but it is also something greater. It is a spiritual something that says, "let go and let the music come of its own accord." Can you create this kind of music - a music that is subtle yet very powerful? A music that can penetrate to the depths yet still remain lovely and light? Yes, you can do it. The secret? Get out of the way and let the music tell you where it wants to go.

After you learn technique and theory and a little bit of improvisation skill, you will be able to grow and create in proportion to your ability to get out of the way and let the music take over. To do this requires a listening ability somewhat similar to meditation. That is, you must be open and receptive to what comes next - never forcing, never trying to come up with something.

When you are in this listening frame of mind, wonderful things begin to happen. But when you try to create something, you set yourself up for blocks. Why? Because the act of trying blocks the listening, receptive attitude necessary for improvisation. The key to getting around this is to walk away and come back later. Believe me, you can try and try but if nothing is coming, it probably won't come at this moment.

Art appears when you are in the moment. The art of New Age piano, like any other art requires you to learn the skills and techniques - then forget about them and begin to play.

Pure Moods:
Playing New Age Piano

Mood music has been popular for a very long time. Way, way before New Age music was established, we've had compositions like "The Planets" by Gustav Holst, "Water Music" by Handel, and "Snowflakes are Dancing" by Claude Debussy.

Of course, it wasn't called "mood music" back then, but people loved the idea of listening to something titled "Grand Canyon Suite" and being led by the music through what the composer experienced. Pieces like "On the Trail" and "Painted Desert" led the listener through the composer's imagination and allowed for a journey into sound.

New Age piano continues this love of descriptive music and has made it's own contributions. CDs like George Winston's "December" are platinum-selling albums because they allow listeners to experience the feeling of walking in snow on a cold winter's day or reminiscing about the upcoming holidays!

The CD, "Yosemite" by Rick Erlien, also celebrates nature's beauty through music and has also been a best seller. It's not surprising. After all, people have loved descriptive music for centuries now!

The great thing about New Age piano is that it's quite easy to learn! Years of studying theory and harmony are not required. In fact, because of its improvisational approach, students can jump right in and begin creating their own unique music right away!

Reduce Stress Through New Age Piano

Y ou've probably heard it before - the calming, tranquil sounds of New Age piano coming from a gift shop or stereo.

There's something about music, especially New Age music that slows the heart rate down. Listening to this kind of music has many therapeutic effects, but did you know that you could also reduce stress by learning how to play in this style? It's true! And the good news is you don't need years of lessons to begin.

All that is required is knowledge of a few chords and that's it! I've had students tell me that nothing relaxes them more than just sitting at the piano and playing what they feel. They aren't concerned with being perfect or "playing it right." They just want to relax, unwind, and forget about their busy day.

The relaxation and sense of well being that comes from playing the piano in the New Age style is profound. Breathing slows down. Focus is sharpened and heightened as well.

Music is a soothing balm and can be very therapeutic and even more so when you actually create it yourself! Reduce stress and feel a sense of peace while you learn how to play chords and make music. It can be done. And it's very easy to begin.

For instance, in the lesson, "Reflections in Water," (available at quiescencemusic.com) you learn how to create a calm, reflective atmosphere using a few chords and the C Major scale. This is something a complete beginner can do and it won't take years, months or weeks. You can improvise and create your own music within hours!

Relaxation Music and New Age Piano

We all need to relax more, and music hath charms to soothe the savage beast. But, have you ever thought that you could create your own relaxation music? Doing so actually has more benefits for you than just listening to it.

Take the piano for example. This instrument is perfect for creating soothing, relaxing ambiences and has been used just for this purpose. There's no need to create bouncy Jazz rhythms or sharp dynamic classical crescendos. On the contrary, the piano can be used to provide a lovely, delicate environment.

The good news is that creating relaxation music is quite easy. All you need are a few chords, a way to play those chords and a scale to improvise from. In fact, if people knew how easy it was, they'd be playing the piano more and more.

For example, let's say you're stressed out and in need of some musical comfort. You go to your piano or keyboard and place your hands on an E Major 7 chord. This could be the beginning of a nice improvisation. You choose a few more chords from the key of E Major and you can now use the music to help you unwind and forget about your busy day.

After a few minutes of playing, you start to feel more relaxed. In fact, it's as if a great weight has been lifted from your shoulders. The music has done its work of soothing and healing and you feel refreshed and more in touch with yourself.

Should Music Be Used for Something?

have this great Japanese flute and koto CD I listen to. It's called Satori and I put it on every once in a while, not to relax, but just to be reminded of what music for music's sake sounds like.

There is no planning here. No forethought. It is pure improvisation and frankly, there is nothing that compares with it as far as being in the moment improvisation is concerned. You can really "feel" the moment here. It's as if time is suspended and there is nothing but the player and the music.

The best thing about this is that you enter the state of mind the musician is in when he recorded the music. You feel, through the music, the feelings and, in this case, the peace the flute player has in his heart as the instrument is played. It's really quite amazing!

Here in the West, we are used to a music that must have a definite beginning and end. Everything is planned out and is designed to produce a certain emotional state. Drums, bass, volume, and heavy production are all used to drive the point home.

But the mind can quickly grow tired of listening to the drone of a digital beat and wants something closer to itself. Something more natural and organic. I can think of no better music to treat the mind to than Japanese flute and koto music.

Showing Up at the Piano

I have a unique philosophy when it comes to piano playing. I don't believe in regular practice. Now, don't get me wrong. If your goal is to become a concert pianist, then regular practice is a must.

But if you're like me and are interested in the experience you get when you sit down and play, then all that is required for you is to "show up" at the piano.

I'm currently working on a new CD project. I set a date for its completion. Now, the problem is, how do I work to complete this project?

Some would set a rigorous agenda to accomplish this. I've tried to do this but it doesn't work for me. I found a better strategy and that is to set time goals.

For example, my minimum goal is to spend at least 15 minutes a day at the piano. My job is to "show up." This approach works very well for me! And it fits in with my philosophy of not forcing anything into being.

I work on a couple of pieces at a time. Sometimes the piece does not want to "go anywhere." It's frustrating sometimes when you have something you want done but it's not going the way you want.

Ideally, I'd love to have the CD finished within a week, but by showing up at my piano every day for the minimum time, I stay true to my philosophy of not forcing a product into creation.

This strategy will not work for everyone, of course. But if you're the kind of person who is more interested in the process, you can use this approach to your advantage if and when you decide to create a CD or some other project.

Six Reasons to Play New Age Piano

Here are six very good reasons to learn how to play piano in the New Age style:

It's easy. No months spent learning theory here. Just a few chords and you're off enjoying the joy of improvisation. Learning chords is the key to playing easily and effortlessly! And with New Age piano, the chords you learn can be used right away!

It's fun! You can actually create your own music! In the classical music world you spend all your time learning how to play other peoples music. With New Age piano, you can sit down and "compose" a piece of your very own.

It sounds good. You can, by using a few modern sounding chords, sound good playing piano right away.

Techniques are easily learned. New Age piano uses techniques that anyone can learn how to play in a matter of minutes.

No note reading involved. New Age piano is very much an improvised music. This being the case, chords are really all that you need to know. Although note reading is nice, it's not necessary in order to create your own music.

It's modern. New Age piano is a modern genre. Having really picked up steam in the mid 1980's, it's something that can grow and become a vital force in today's society.

Stress Relief and Music

Stress. It affects us all. The noise. The emotional upsets. The rapidly approaching holiday season that we're all supposed to smile our way through.

Thankfully, one of the ways we can relieve stress is by putting on some relaxing music. Some love to listen to nature sounds. Some quiet piano music. Whatever you are attracted to, take a minute to sit down, close your eyes, and listen.

Your heart rate and breathing will start to slow down along with your thoughts. As you tune in to the sound of the music, you let go of the cares and concerns of the outer world. Now, an inner journey begins to take place.

After listening for a few minutes, you find yourself feeling refreshed and renewed, as if a blanket of sound has washed you clean. And all you had to do was put a CD in your player. Listening to music is a great way to reduce stress levels. Playing music can actually reduce stress even further.

As we approach our chosen instrument, we settle into a happy routine that always brings us comfort and joy. As a piano player, I love preparing to play. The act of sliding the bench out, of touching the keys and placing my hands on a chord all contribute to a calming ritual that allows me to relax and unwind. And then as I play, the cares and concerns of this world slowly drop off my shoulders. I am transported into a place where peace is present.

The 2 Styles of New Age Piano Playing

Believe it or not, there is actually a hard and a soft way to play New Age piano. Two different "schools", or styles, have made their appearance in the last 20 years or so.

The first style made popular by George Winston introduces a more percussive "hard" sound. Created mostly by a left hand ostinato, this style is very chord-oriented and paints a background of textures while the right hand is free to improvise a melody. The reason that I say this style is a hard sounding one is that when compared with someone like David Lanz, the difference is readily apparent.

Lanz goes for a softer, more melodic approach. This isn't to say that either of these artists has never played in different ways, it's just that their signature sound is different.

As an example, look at the piece, "Rainforest." It is a percussive piece made up of a left hand ostinato pattern. Now the piece, "Ocean Dreams," is softer with the melody actually taking center stage.

It's a good idea to familiarize yourself with both styles. When I first started playing, I identified mostly with the "Winston" style but find myself leaning more towards a softer style now. I really like the pianist, John Herberman, from the Solitude's label. His playing is exquisite and very emotional.

The Artist's Way Meets the Piano

In her bestselling book, "*The Artist's Way*," Julie Cameron suggests keeping a journal. She refers to them as morning pages where each morning, you just write off the top of your head.

This free writing exercise is nothing new. It's been done and popularized for quite some time now. But "*The Artist's Way*" really brought this practice back.

I was wondering why musicians, specifically piano players, might apply the concept of free writing to playing piano.

It then dawned on me that if you time your improvisations, or more accurately, set a time limit for how long you're going to play, it creates a space where the muse is free to express.

To this end, I created a lesson titled "Timed Piano Improvisation Exercise." It is a lesson that uses a three to five minute time limit. Students are encouraged to play whatever comes up within the given parameters - three chords in the mode of A Aeolian.

The beauty of these kinds of exercises is that the choice as to what to play has already been made. All that is required is for the student to sit down and play within the limits set.

Some fight the idea of limitations, thinking it constricts creativity. Not true! It actually helps you to focus on self-expression. That's because you're not thinking about the next chord to play. This choice has already been made. All that is required now is to simply create in the moment.

When the moment is a timed practice period, it gives students the freedom to just be at the piano.

After successfully trying these exercises myself, I realize how powerful they can be. Material comes that may have never appeared any other way. Why? Because we aren't focused on creating a product. Instead, we allow the improvisational process to lead us and this always leads to the "freshest" sounding music.

The Beauty of New Age Piano

There are so many styles of music out there. Thankfully, there is also New Age piano music. A wonderful style of playing that goes right to the heart bringing back memories, feelings, and emotions, or creating new pictures in our heads. Impressionistic in nature, New Age piano music does not seek to try and tell you something. Instead, it leads the listener on a journey.

For instance, the lesson, "Autumn," was created by looking at a picture that inspired me. A few minutes later, that piece was created. This is the beauty of New Age piano. It's a style of music that doesn't take long to learn and can be experienced quickly. A few chords, a sound, a technique are all that is needed and we are off exploring a world of sound.

George Winston, the man who literally put New Age piano on the map, looks at his music as a soundtrack for the seasons. He loves the idea of giving voice to the natural world. Visual artists have been doing this for hundreds of years. Monet, Manet, and other French impressionists interpreted how they felt about the natural world through paint and composition.

Music also has it's impressionistic counterpart. Claude Debussy, certainly one of the greatest composers of the 20th century, based many of his compositions on nature themes. And now we have New Age piano -a contemporary, and I think quite necessary, art form that seeks to infuse the beauty of nature with music!

The Flower Garden and New Age Piano Music

If you've ever looked at a flower garden, not only its beauty may have captivated you, but also its overall arrangement.

There may have been some tulips or roses combined with other flowers or plants.

You may also have stood there looking it over. Maybe you started on one side and your eye moved down or vice-versa. Now, music making is a lot like flower arranging. You combine different elements to make a pleasing whole.

It is a natural tendency of the human mind to create order out of chaos and art from nothing. What is pleasing to the listening ear is symmetry. The flower arrangement captivates, not only because of its great beauty, but because it has been composed and arranged to a pleasing whole - something the eye and the mind can grasp hold of and ponder.

We walk away with a sense of completion because someone took the time to bring order into chaos. Someone arranged varying elements to create art. This is what musicians do whether they realize it or not. But instead of flowers, we use notes and chords. Instead of a vase, we use musical form to hold the notes and chords.

Music is a more difficult art because the elements are not as easily put together. Music is slippery and ephemeral but when we learn to use the tools of repetition and contrast, we begin to put some order into chaos. Chaos is good and has its place in improvisation, however, for those who wish to compose their own music, it's a good idea to learn the tools of the trade.

The flower arranger must know how to create a balance between color and form to create the overall look and feel of the arrangement. The composer must also create balance but uses musical materials - chords, notes, phrases, etc.

Then, he puts it together into a framework. A flower arrangement can be big or small depending on the size of the vase. Similarly, a new age piano work can be long or short depending on the amount of contrast and repetition used.

The Horror of Traditional Piano Lessons

Now that Halloween is over, it's safe to talk about traditional piano lessons - the tedium, the boredom, the overbearing teachers with their incessant metronome beats.

Do we really need this? Do we really need yet another polished perfomer who can play Czerny and Beethoven on cue? Don't we have enough of these skilled typists already? I think so. And frankly, I just don't get it. I don't get why anyone would want to learn how to play other people's music.

Of course this music is worthy of preserving, but I'm speaking about being creative at the piano. I'm talking about the ability to sit down at the keyboard and just play without forethought or planning.

Is there value in this kind of approach to playing? Yes! And while improvisation and composition are taught, it's not emphasized. It's relegated to inferior status while the poor student spends time first learning how to read notes and then recreating what has already been done. What a shame.

It doesn't have to be this way. We can lead with an emphasis on creativity first! To do this does not require more than a very rudimentary knowledge of chords, a way to play them, and a guided instruction on how to improvise. Imagine the joy students will feel when they realize how easy it is to create music!

The Magic of New Age Piano

Appealing and attractive, the New Age piano genre has become welcomed into the homes of millions of people around the world. And, why not? It's a beautiful music that has an honest, heartfelt approach.

It's easy to create on your own! No extensive theory or training is required to play what you feel. On the contrary, a few chords and a simple melody are all that is necessary and the complete beginner can start creating music.

For example, in the lesson "Flower Garden," we have three chords to play - C Major 9, B flat Major 9, and A flat Major 9. We have a technique that we use throughout the improvisation called the crossover technique. Here we use the left hand to create a harmonic backdrop over which the right hand improvises a melody. A simple and effective approach to creating music, this harmonic loop is repeated over and over while the melody is improvised and changed around to keep the music fresh.

All of this is played over a 16 bar framework. The chord changes come every few bars and this is indicated on the chord chart. It's an easy map to follow.

These simple materials are used to create music with. In

fact, you could actually create complete pieces of music using these materials alone!

The magic and beauty of the New Age piano style is that it offers the beginning piano student an accessible approach to the world of improvisation and composition. The music itself is quite appealing and has firmly established itself in the musical repertoire of the world.

The New Age Piano Style - What Does It Offer?

Mention the name George Winston and most people immediately think of New Age piano. He pretty much cornered the sound most of us equate with "New Age."

Ask people what they like about this music and most will say, "It relaxes me," or "It helps me unwind." Both perfectly fine reasons for liking music.

For some reason, relaxation and peaceful seem to be words many would rather not associate with music. These people want music to be exciting and vibrant and there is nothing at all wrong with this. But the world is big enough to contain many genres.

New Age, Jazz, and Classical are all categories thought up by marketing executives to make the selling process easier. Unfortunately, it also lumps music that otherwise might have been heard by many, into a category where only a few have the opportunity to listen to it.

New Age piano music has much to offer not only the listener, but the performer as well. Going way past stress-reduction, playing the piano in this style enables one to feel a deep sense of well-being. When one is able to improvise and be in the moment, it becomes a very rare, and beautiful experience.

The Simple Joy Of New Age Piano Playing

Ah ... to sit down and play. So many want to be able to just go to the piano and play what they feel.

Traditionally, Jazz has been the champion of improvisational music. Students who want to express themselves creatively know that jazz is an art form that encourages improvisation.

But then there's New Age music. A genre that has not been around as long as Jazz, but one that embraces the improvisational approach as well. The great thing about New Age piano playing is that it's much easier to get into than jazz!

The typical jazz pianist spends many hours studying chords and scales with the hopes of one day being able to freely express at the piano. Much technique and understanding is required before students are usually encouraged to go ahead and "let loose."

Not New Age piano. In fact, this style is attractive specifically because most people can just sit down at the piano right away and start improvising and creating music.

This is possible because New Age piano does not require lengthy study of technique and harmony. On the contrary, a complete beginner can use just 2 chords and begin playing music right away.

For example, in the author's lesson "Winter Scene," we have two chords and a scale to learn. That's it! And once these things are understood, the student can begin expressing through music right away.

The myth that you need to know a lot before diving into music is just that - a myth. All that is required is an attitude of exploration and a willingness to try.

What Happened to New Age Piano?

I t all began in the early 1980's with a recording titled "December." The artist was George Winston and for some strange reason, people really liked it. The music was different. It seemed to go nowhere and float on the air. No matter. People liked it.

Then something peculiar happened. Marketing executives at various record labels didn't know what to call it. After all, this music needed some kind of label or classification to sell it to the public but what? Then some idiot came up with the name, "New Age," and the genre has suffered ever since. Even George Winston hates the term and calls his piano music "rural folk."

But, and here's the really weird thing, lots of people really like this music! Unfortunately, many were turned off by the New Age thing. It's true. They liked the music but just didn't want anything to do with anything with New Age (whatever that is). I've even had someone email me saying they liked my sample lessons but didn't want to sign up for fear of being labeled New Age.

New Age piano is just a style of music. It has nothing to do with philosophy. It has nothing to do with religion. It's just a style of music like zydeco or polka music. You either like it or you don't.

It's a shame to let such a beautiful and worthy thing as New Age piano fall to the wayside because of labels.

What is New Age Piano Anyway?

Having played what is commonly called "New Age Piano" for the last 16 years, you'd think I'd be qualified to define it. But I'll be perfectly honest with you and say I haven't the slightest clue!

Here's what I know. I know the music is more consonant than dissonant. I know that the harmonies are mostly major but can be minor and that chord choice leans towards a "clean" sound. As far as melody goes, it can be anything from an ambient mélange with no discernible direction to a simple folk spun line a child could follow.

Now that the basic elements of music are out of the way, I really couldn't tell you what makes New Age Piano "New Age."

Is it the relaxing aspect of this music that makes it "New

Age?" Perhaps, but then classical music is also quite relaxing and soothing as well. Is it the artists themselves who play this music? Maybe, but speaking personally, I can tell you that I don't practice a "New Age" religion -whatever that is and I don't believe in much of what is espoused as "New Age" philosophy. As a matter of fact, I don't even know what "New Age" philosophy is, but I'm guessing that it's anything besides what mainstream religion/philosophy is.

So what makes New Age music New Age? I don't really know. I can only tell you that when it came time to market these CDs to the world, executives in marketing realized the music would sell better if it were under a different umbrella than say, jazz or classical. I imagine they came up with the term, "New Age," for the soothing qualities much of this music has. Which is fine by me.

Zen and the
Art of New Age Piano

We all want to be in the moment. That's where real transformation takes place. For some, walking gets them there. Others like to play sports or watch movies. For me, it's playing the piano. When I'm in the moment, letting the music speak, it's like the world is new again.

The notes flow out of the piano into the air and I know that something magical is taking place. It may last a minute or a half-hour. No matter how long it lasts, I know that I've been transported to a special place. Many musicians know of this place - especially musicians who know how to improvise. There is no planning - only spontaneous invention.

Zen music in particular has an ethereal quality that seems to grow organically. It starts and ends yet there seems to be no starting or ending point. The music just *is* - like a living being it is just there. It's like a fine perfume in the sense that it lingers in the air but does not overwhelm or grow tiresome.

Any instrument can be used to create this kind of music but certain instruments lend themselves more readily to it. Flutes, the harp, the piano, the Japanese Koto - these instruments are often used to create atmospheres that linger delightfully but really do not want to go anywhere. Here in the West, we are used to a music that must pursue an ending course. We must have a climax or a big finish or we are not satisfied. Like a fireworks show, it begins and ends with a bang.

There can be a struggle between creating a music that comes from spirit or making music that pleases the crowd. We can be torn between pleasing the ego or pleasing ourselves. To play piano in the "new age" style is to understand a music that isn't planned but allowed to become. Once this concept is understood, the music will flow.

Technique

Amazing Technique for New Age Piano Lets You Create Rich Harmonic Backgrounds

When I first heard the piece, "Rain," by George Winston I was blown away. Here was a solo piano piece that sounded so rich and full, you could swear more than one person was playing it. Yet it's just one man on one piano.

When Winston released his video, I got to see how he did it. It all has to do with the left hand. He uses the left hand to create a beautiful ostinato pattern. But this is no ordinary pattern. The secret to how he gets his sound is in the thumb. You see he moves the thumb back and forth past an octave to add in more notes. Not too complicated once you understand how it's done.

Once the ostinato pattern is "down" in the left hand, the right comes in with the melody. The trick to creating something like this is to really get the pattern down first in the left hand. There's a lot you can do here - even with two chords!

After the left hand is secure and the right comes in with improvised melody, Winston does something else that mystifies those who've never seen it. He reaches over his left hand with the right to hit bass notes. In my lesson, "Flashflood," I use the same technique. I take two chords (E flat Major and

B Major) and use them to full advantage.

This really adds to the whole thing. Sonorous, thunderous bass notes create an added richness. And one person is still doing it all. It really is amazing.

Arpeggios and New Age Piano Playing

Chopin used arpeggios extensively. So did Beethoven and Mozart. They are beautiful and perfect for the New Age piano style too!

You can hear arpeggios in George Winston's music. David Lanz uses them in many of his compositions, and of course, I use them as well. Why? Because the piano is well suited for this technique!

The left hand is used mostly to create this cascading flow of notes. For example, in the lesson, "Wood Thrush," we use over two octaves of the keyboard. This creates a very nice background over which we can improvise (or compose) our melodies.

Because the New Age piano style focuses a lot on improvisation, the arpeggio is an excellent vehicle to use. We pick a key to play in, choose a few chords from that key, then create an arpeggio with them.

What gives many students problems with this technique is the crossover part where the left hand does its main work. But once this technique is mastered, the rest is easy.

Then, you simply practice playing the arpeggio until you

can improvise a melody in your right hand. You go slowly and smoothly at first, not rushing, but taking your time. The rewards are great because the sound that is created by using arpeggios is full, rich, and very appealing to the ear!

Basic Piano Lessons - Introducing The Open Position Chord

So many people want to learn the piano. Usually, this means one of two things - they want to learn classical repertoire or they want to be able to read from "fake" books and play pop standards. Both are worthy goals.

But basic piano lessons can be so much more than that.

What if you could create your own unique music at the piano without years of study? In fact, by learning how to play the open position piano chord, you can actually create your own music in as little as one hour! Think this is absurd? Read on...

The open position chord is a special way of forming chords on the keyboard. Instead of triads as your first intro-duction to piano chords, you get to form modern sounding chords using both hands right away.

In fact, you can play all of the open position chords in the key of C Major within 30 minutes. Now, all of these chords are located on the white keys and this makes it very easy. But once you learn this chord position, playing it in the other 11 keys is quite simple.

The thing about basic piano lessons that's bothered so

many for so long is that they are, for the most part, BORING!

Usually, you learn how to form triads and play songs like Kum Ba Ya. And this takes complete beginners days if not weeks to do.

There is a better way and it really starts with the kinds of chords you begin to use first at the piano. There's absolutely no reason to begin your study of the piano with triads. The open position chord will allow you to create a modern sound very quickly. And if you want to play from fake books, this chord will serve you nicely as well.

If you're thinking about learning piano, try learning the open position chord structure first. You won't be disappointed.

Beyond the Open Position Piano Chord

Those of you who have been reading my articles for some time know that I'm a big fan of the open position chord. This is where both hands play a chord together. It's a great technique that allows beginners (and pros) sound good at the piano right away. But, it's just one method or way to approach chord piano playing.

Another method I use is something called the crossover technique or arpeggio. Here the left hand plays a cascade of notes ascending or descending (usually ascending) while the right hand plays melody. This technique is especially suited for New Age piano playing because we can get a gentle flow of notes in the left hand. In fact, you can use over two octaves just in the left hand. This covers a lot of musical space so to speak and creates a lovely backdrop over which melodies may be composed or improvised.

For example, in the lesson, "Winter Sky," we have a 16-bar phrase in the key of B flat. The chords are charted out for you and you can hear me playing the left-hand crossover pattern. This pattern uses much of the left hand right away. The right hand plays octave melody notes and the whole piece is finished in a few minutes.

Usually, when we use the open position chord, we skip the third in the left hand. In this lesson, we use the third to create a denser sound. And it works out well! When you block out or chart the chords using the crossover technique, you create a harmonic background, a canvas of sound over which you paint in your foreground using melody instead of paint! A unique, but very helpful way of seeing how an improvisation or composition can be structured!

Breakthrough Chord Structure Makes Playing Piano a Breeze!

D o you know why playing guitar is so much easier than playing piano? It's because guitar players learn how to use chords first. Even before note reading!

They usually learn how to play chords in the first position. Called open position chords, the beginning guitarist quickly learns how to finger this position and can immediately create music. That's why so many people love the guitar and want to learn it!

They don't waste time learning "the masters" or anything like that at all. Nope. It's all contemporary. Unless of course, it's classical guitar.

Now why can't those interested in learning piano have the same benefits? After all, it's not like everyone wants to learn how to play Bach or Beethoven.

The good news is you can play piano using only chords. But not just any chords. I'm talking about learning a chord structure that will have you sounding like a professional right away! It's called the Open Position Chord and with it, you'll be able to create your own unique music!

I know it sounds far-fetched. I didn't think I could make my own music either until I discovered this chord position from a book titled "*The Four-Way Keyboard System.*" In it, the author Alan Swain goes into great detail about the benefits of learning this chord structure.

I didn't have to really read what he wrote. I just played it. And I was hooked! Here was something I could learn quite easily. And I could learn it in all 12 keys just as easily! I had found what I was looking for. A modern sounding chord that would let me improvise with both hands at the piano right away AND sound good doing it!

Most of us know what triads are. This 3-note chord structure has been used to introduce students to chording on the piano. But learning triads isn't necessarily the best place to start. In fact, there really is no good reason to begin your piano studies with triads.

Listen, if your goal is to read music and play kum-ba-ya, then by all means, spend countless hours learning how to read music and play triads. But, if you want to improvise and create your own unique music, I can think of no better chord structure than the open position chord!

Breathing Space in Music

While most students want to know when to play certain notes and chords, it's equally important to know when not to play. For example, I had a student who knew how to improvise and play in the New Age style. What he didn't know how to do was to allow for breathing space. I tried to teach him that you don't have to play note upon note but allow for some pauses.

Eventually he got it. He learned how not to rush and that the pauses between notes are as important as the notes themselves - especially in the New Age style of piano playing. Listen to pioneer New Age piano player, Steven Halpern, to get an excellent idea of this. Steven literally defined "breathing space" for music. His music floats in the air. It is pure improvisation and, if you listen to him play, you'll find that it's one of the easiest styles in which to play.

He lets the spaces between the notes work for him. There's definitely no rushing here. It's very trance inducing and calming. To play in this way, you need to be very much IN THE PRESENT and listen for what's to come. There's no planning or forethought here except maybe to choose a key or mode to play in. Then you just improvise.

The spaces between the music are as important as the music itself. In fact, without the spaces, you wouldn't have this style. The spaces define the style of music. A lot of New Age pianists emulated Halpern and you can't do better to learn how to master the art of silence than by listening to him. Also, check out the author's online piano lesson, "Oriental Sunrise." to get another good example of "breathing space."

Broken Chord Piano Technique:
"What It is and How to Use It"

Ah, broken chords. The sound. The cascading pattern of chordal notes. It's beautiful. There's no doubt about it. And this technique is one of the easiest to learn. After all, all you need to do to create it is have a chord under your fingers and be able to "break it up."

What do I mean by break it up? You've probably heard of solid chords. This is when all tones are heard at once. For example, if I finger a C Major triad and play all three keys at once, I'm playing a solid chord. But, if I break this chord up into it's three notes and play them one at a time you get a broken chord.

Broken chords are used frequently in New Age piano music. There's something about playing notes of a chord in broken style that's very appealing. Maybe it's because it makes the piano sound fuller. Or it could be that it just sounds lovely.

Now, let's take a look at how we can easily create it.

In the lesson, "Reflections in Water," we have four open position chords. These chords are ideal for "breaking up" because they are so wide-spaced. Over two octaves of notes lay under your fingertips. Once we finger this chord position we are able to play the broken-chord style. How? By simply letting your fingers play around with the note possibilities! And there are many of them.

When you listen to me play this piece, you'll notice that it's nothing to write home about. That is, I'm not after a "sophisticated" sound here. I'm just gently playing around with the notes and using the element of time to create a calm ambiance. And it works! The notes float out into the air and music is created. Not by planning or trying to come up with material but by following a few simple guidelines and letting go of the need to control the outcome.

Chord Piano - An Easy Way to Begin

Do you know why the guitar is the most popular instrument in the world? It's because it's easy for a complete beginner to pick it up and actually create something most of us can call music right away.

Do you think a beginning piano student can do this? Not really. That's why learning how to play chord piano is becoming so popular. <u>Most students don't want to wait years before they can create music.</u> They want to be creative like their guitarist counterparts - and why not?

Learning how to play chord piano is actually easier then playing chords on a guitar. It's because you don't have to hurt your fingers on the strings. No finger calluses here. Not at all. In fact, the piano may be the easiest of all instruments to play. Just press on a key and you've sounded a note. Press on three or more keys and you have created a chord.

Now, when most beginners think of playing piano chords, their minds immediately turn to triads. While triads are OK and are frequently played in most music, it's not the best chord structure to start out with. This is because we do not live in the 19th century anymore! Most piano students want to learn something that sounds a little closer to the century we're living in and this is where the open position chord structure comes in.

This modern sounding 6-note chord covers more than two octaves of the piano making it the best starting place for the beginner to create modern sounds. It is a seventh chord too! Used frequently in Jazz and New Age music, this chord type is easily modifiable into larger chord extensions as well.

Don't let guitarists have all the fun. Learn chord piano and you'll soon be the envy of guitar players everywhere!

Chord Progressions for New Age Piano

The sound of New Age music can be divided into the three parts melody, harmony, and rhythm. The harmony aspect can be thought of simply as chords. New Age music does use certain piano chords more than others.

One chord I'm fond of is the 9th chord. All this means is that the ninth note of the scale is used to create the chord with. For example, a triad built from the C Major scale is spelled -c-e-g. If we add the seventh note in the scale (b) we get a seventh chord - C Major 7. It's spelled -c-e-g-b. Simple enough.

Now if we continue up the scale we will hit the octave C. The next note after this is the 9th note (d). It's also the 2nd note in the scale. This can get confusing but it's just a system of counting. The C Major 9 chord is spelled c-e-g-b-d. This chord has a very rich sound and is used often in New Age music. It can be used as an ostinato, or as broken chord or arpeggio.

A typical New Age chord progression is simple and usually stays within the scale it came from. We can play C Major, F Major. and G Major. and by using just these three piano chords, improvise and create in the New Age style.

In fact, in the online lesson, "Ocean Dreams," this is exactly what is done. Except in this lesson, I eliminate the seventh tone from the chord and play an octave in the left hand.

By eliminating the seventh tone, I'm creating a more folksy or New Age sound. The seventh tone is used mainly in Jazz music but can be used in New Age music as well.

Once the left hand is "down," I add in tones from the C Major scale, especially the ninth tone (d) and the New Age sound is apparent.

Czerny, Finger Exercises, and Piano Playing

When I first began playing piano... now over 16 years ago, I thought the best way to begin was to read music and play simple finger exercises so I could get used to the instrument.

Turns out I was just a little right. Some of Czerny's exercises are very good for developing finger strength and dexterity. When I have nothing better to do, I'll practice five note finger patterns on the white keys.

But now, I don't practice scales, exercises or any other kind of "technique" exercise. Why? Because I've discovered a better way to warm up and get the fingers going. Of course I'm speaking about improvisation. You know, the great thing about improvisation is that technique is invented when it is required.

Learning rote fingering will never make you a good piano player. Trusting your intuition and letting your fingers guide you will serve you much better.

Using finger exercises to warm up is not a bad idea at all, but will not give you the dexterity and adeptness that just improvising will. This is because the former way is rote while the latter is spontaneous creation. From moment to moment, the fingers will follow the heart and will lead you to new combinations and ways to express. In fact, through improvisation, you'll come up with entirely new fingerings!

Extremely Simple Way to Play What You Feel on the Piano - Even if You've Never Played Before!

How would you like to be able to play what you feel on the piano within one hour? Impossible? Not at all. It's all about chords. But not just any chord structure.

The chord structure I'm talking about will have you playing the piano with both hands right away. And it won't take hours or days to do it. I'm talking about something called the open position chord, and with it, you'll be able to really create your own music!

The trick to all this is how the chord is made. You see, most piano teachers begin their students with triads. And while there is nothing wrong with learning triads, they're a little antiquated.

The open position chord is a <u>modern sounding seventh chord</u> that is used today in pop, jazz, new age, and other contemporary piano styling. The seventh chord is a term that is used to describe how the chord is constructed. It's really easy. The chord is made up of the root note, the third, the fifth, and the seventh. If we were playing a C Major 7 chord, it would be spelled c-e-g-b.

Now, by itself, the seventh chord is a very good and often used chord structure. But, if we "open it up" by breaking the chord up into both hands, we get a very spacious and beautiful sounding chord... hence the name open position. Here's how it's constructed. The left hand gets the root note, the fifth, and the seventh. The right hand plays the third, the seventh and the third again. Spelled out, this would be: Left hand... c-g-b. Right hand... e-b-e.

This six-note chord sounds unbelievably full and rich. And the best thing about it? Once you get this chord down in your hands, you can learn how to play it very easily in all 12 keys!

George Winston Music - Create it Easily Yourself!

You're looking for some music by George Winston, huh? Of course you are! Winston's music is timeless, bringing together the beauty of the natural world and piano into one gorgeous aural canvas.

George has been creating this kind of music for over 20 years. But have you ever wanted to play the piano like George? You can. And it's a lot easier than you might think. For instance, what George does on the keyboard is not that complicated. It can sound complicated yes, but once you understand what's going on, you too can create like this.

Most of George's compositions revolve around a left-hand ostinato pattern. This simply means "repeating pattern" and is perfect for the New Age style of playing. In fact, George has said in a Rolling Stone interview exactly what he does. I'm paraphrasing here … "What I do is get the left hand down. It does its thing and is like the background of a band. Then the right hand comes in and improvises melody. The right hand gets freer and freer."

And that pretty much sums up how some of George's music is created. What I have most of my students do at first is learn something called the open position chord. This allows you to play modern sounding chords with both hands right away! Once this chord structure is mastered, you can pretty much do anything you want on the keyboard. This is possible because you learn how to make the most of both hands immediately.

A good example of this chord structure in action comes from the lesson, "Reflections in Water" (available at quiescencemusic.com). This lesson is an improvisation exercise in the key of C Major. It's all on the white keys making for a very easy experience for the beginning (and advanced) piano student.

I show you how to play this 6-note chord structure all the way up the C Major scale. Once this is understood, you can literally begin creating your own music right away. And in the video, you'll see exactly how to do it. Nothing complicated at all about this. You play certain chords from the Key of C Major and improvise your own unique melody from the C Major scale.

Once you start playing like this, it may be hard to stop!

How to Figure Out What Another Pianist is Doing

A student once asked me, "Can I determine what my favorite piano player is actually doing on the keyboard just by listening?" It's an excellent question and one that can be answered in the affirmative. **Here's how to do it.**

First, figure out what the left hand is doing. This is the key to understanding what is being done by any piano player, no matter what the style. Let's take New Age pianist David Lanz as an example. Lanz's style usually revolves around a left hand that plays an ostinato pattern while the right hand improvises. Very few pianists base their compositions on the right hand.

It has to do with the way the piano is structured. You have the bass notes and midrange section of the keyboard allotted to the left hand. And this accounts for the "arrangement" of most piano pieces. In fact, once you figure out what the left hand is doing, you've got it down for most pieces!

The left hand will usually be playing an arpeggio, broken or solid chords, or bass-chord arrangement. The right hand will be playing melody and/or harmonizing the melody with chords.

For example, if we listen to the piece, "Thanksgiving," by George Winston, we notice right away a harmonic background being played. Now for the novice listener, all they may hear is notes and not know what is being done. But nine times out of ten, the accompaniment of a piano piece is taken by the left hand and that is exactly what is happening in this piece. Then the right hand comes in to play a melody and this turns out to be the arrangement for the entire piece.

Of course, there are many exceptions to the left hand rule as when the right hand hits notes and chords while the left hand plays bass. If you listen for what the left hand is doing, you can figure out how most solo piano pieces are constructed.

How to Jump Chords Up the Keyboard to Create a Free-Flowing Sound!

Chord jumping is a simple technique that allows you to use much of the piano. You simply take a chord and "move it" up the keyboard.

Now, I'm not talking about inversions here, although there's nothing wrong with inversions. I'm talking about taking a simple chord structure and just using the entire piano to create with. Here's what I mean.

Take the lesson, "Coral Reef," for example. Here we have two chords, A minor and F Major. The beauty of only having two chords for this improvisation exercise is that it frees you to experiment. That is, you can focus on moving them around instead of looking to see when the chords change.

Here you use your two chords and change them whenever you want. The left hand is playing an octave (open position) while the right hand is free to play melody. And the sound created from this is fantastic. In fact, to the untrained ear, you never would know that just two chords are used. But it's true.

The thing about chords and playing them is that **the magic really unfolds when you limit choice** (use only two chords and have a certain technique to play them) and let your intuition guide you. Then you can finally forget about thinking and actually experience the music firsthand. This is a place of pure improvisation and inspiration where your intuition guides you.

There is no thinking, no wondering what to do. Now, instead of trying to make the music go somewhere, you let go and allow the music to tell you where it wants to go... a subtle but necessary shift if you want to experience all that music making and improvisation has to offer you.

How to Quickly Play Piano Using the Incredible Open Position Chord!

Imagine being able to sit down at the piano and create your own unique music without years of study. Now imagine being able to do it within one hour! It's possible when you learn how to play the open position piano chord!

The OPC is a special way of forming chords at the piano. You use both hands right away to create a modern sounding chord that's perfect for today's contemporary styles. It's called "open position" because of the way the notes of the chord are spread out.

The left hand plays the root, fifth, and seventh notes of the chord while the right hand takes the third and seventh again. The sound is amazing but this isn't the biggest benefit of this particular chord structure. The biggest benefit is what you can do with it!

For example, in the piano lesson, "Reflections in Water," you start by playing a C Major 7 OPC. Now that you have the chord, what are you going to do to make music? You are going to improvise a melody with the right hand using the tones from the C Major scale. You see, all you really need to know in order to make your own music is chords and the scale the chords came from.

You need to know the notes of the scale so you can use them to improvise a melody. Now the beauty of the open position chord is that you don't have to move your hands around too much in order to create a melody. In fact, you can pretty much stay within this chord structure and create a beautiful piece of music.

Reflections in Water uses four chords to create a few minutes of music. A beginner can learn to use this chord structure within one hour and create music with it. It really is that easy! How to Use an Ostinato Pattern to Make Your Piano Playing Sound Incredible!

Did you know there are only a few patterns used on the piano? For example, there's the arpeggio, the bass-chord technique, crossed hands, and of course, the ostinato.

What's so special about the ostinato pattern? It's very easy to use! We take a chord (or an arpeggio) and create a loop with it. This allows the right hand to freely improvise melody. Even a complete beginner can get a simple chord pattern down. For instance, in the lesson, "Winter Scene," we have two chords. Just two chords is all we need to create a very pleasant harmonic background over which we "paint" our melodies!

It doesn't have to get more complicated than this for an absolute beginner (or pro) to experience the joy of improvisation. The chords used for this lesson are modern sounding and are used frequently in both jazz and new age piano music. We take this four-note chord and break it up creating a lovely textural sound. We vary the dynamics (loud and soft) to make our playing more musical and from this we get two or more minutes of music!

It's all done with chords. Chords and phrases. Actually, "Winter Scene" is simply a 4-bar phrase repeated a number of times. By thinking "in phrases" the improviser/composer learns how to use the art of repetition and contrast to advantage. No longer thinking in just chords, it becomes easier to block out entire sections of music quickly and easily!

How to Use the
Entire Piano Keyboard

There are 88 keys on the piano keyboard. Most pianists use about 1/3 of this number most of the time. Why?

Well, if you're playing sheet music, the answer lies in how the composer used the piano. If you're creating your own music, the answer lies in experimenting with the possibilities.

Most of my own music is played near the middle of the keyboard. It's not planned that way but this is the area of the piano I naturally gravitate towards when sitting down to play. Of course, I do and have used most notes available on the piano and it would be a shame not to. But I allow the music to tell me where it wants to go. If I sit down with a predetermined agenda to play high notes, then I am not listening to my intuition.

Although I have to admit that in lesson 5, "Winter Scene," I wanted to create a crisp wintry sound so I started farther up the keyboard with the left hand and played higher register notes in my right. But most times, I will let my intuition guide me and nine times out of 10 begin at the middle of the keyboard.

There is nothing wrong or uncreative about this at all. In fact, it doesn't really matter where you begin because once started, the heart and mind work together as one bringing you the ideal music. It is the only true music that could come out of you because you listen to what your heart wants to play. If you play a few bass notes to begin with fine. Want to start at the high end of the piano, OK.

The key here is authenticity. Some compositions and improvisations sound contrived because they were - that is they were thought up. There really is nothing wrong per se with this approach as long as you let the music guide you. For example, you may decide you want to do as I did and create a certain mood piece. However, once you get the general idea for the music, let it guide you to where it wants to go - that is, listen, listen, listen for what is coming next. This approach never fails and will most always yield good results.

It's Easy to Create Melody!

Some consider melody the most important aspect of music making. Of course, there's harmony and rhythm, but melody is the one part that listeners hold to memory more than any other. It's also the easiest part to create!

For example, in the lesson, "Oriental Sunrise," we have two chords. Now if we just play these chords, if we just fool around with them, we get textures and whiffs of sound that drift away and do not hold. But, as soon as we add in melody, the whole piece becomes alive and discernable.

To create a melody really requires nothing more than playing around with the right hand. The left has the chords and creates the harmonic background - an aural canvas, if you will. Now, we can add in highlights to our sound painting using melody.

We improvise and are amazed at the fact that just a few notes is enough to create a wonderful sound - especially since you use the pentatonic scale. You can't go wrong by playing on the black keys. Every note you produce will sound "good." We let go and allow our intuitive mind to come up with the melody and the music pours out of us.

Once you know the scale you'll be playing in, (in this case, minor pentatonic) you are free to play any note you want from it to create your melody. The focus is now on making music and not on choosing melody notes - a very freeing experience!

Just 3 Chords? No Way!

A student wrote me an email about the lesson, "Ocean Dreams." Here it is:

"Dear Edward, I can't believe that you're using just three chords for this piece. It sounds like it uses much more material. Please tell me how you did it!"

Here's my answer –

Dear B.,

First, thanks for listening to my free lesson. To answer your question, the secret to getting the full sound you hear in this piece is not in how many chords are used. It's in how the chord is voiced! Notice in the lesson that your left hand is very much open and covers a full octave of the keyboard.

This is what creates the full sound you hear! My right hand is playing melody notes pretty close to the left. Also, I use the principles of repetition and contrast to maintain interest. For example, you'll notice that there is a beginning section where the melody repeats. Then another section is added (still only using the same three chords) with a contrasting melody. Then back to the first theme so the whole piece can be broken down into what's commonly know as

ABA form (even though this piece was improvised).

Using repetition and contrast, we create music that has a definable form or shape. ABA form is very, very common and is used in almost all genres of music, especially New Age. This is why I always say that you don't need a lot of material to create with. If you understand and use time-tested principles, you can use just three chords and create an entire piece of music. I hope this answers your question.

Regards, Edward Weiss.

Learn Piano Chords
The Easy Way!

So, you're thinking about (or are already) playing piano using the chord approach. But, you're lost in the sea of chord types.

There are minor piano chords, major piano chords, and diminished piano chords. There are 9th chords, flat 5 chords, and other chords I can't even begin to describe to you.

The good news is you don't need to learn piano chords this way. There's a much easier way to learn them and it all has to do with something called the open position chord.

Those of you who have been reading my articles for some time know I'm a big fan of this chord structure. You also know that I like it because you use both hands right away to create a modern sounding seventh chord.

Now why is starting out with seventh chords so important? Because, this chord type is the foundation for ALL modern chords period.

By starting with this chord structure and learning all the chords in all 12 keys, you have a foundation to build on.

This way it won't confuse you. For example, in the key of C Major we have 7 chords. These are: C Major 7, D minor 7, E minor 7, F Major 7, G7, A minor 7, and B diminished 7. The last chord (B diminished seven is rarely used) but is included for you anyway.

Once you learn these chords in the key of C Major, you simply go down the circle of fifths. The next key is F Major and so on.

By learning only seventh chords to start, it makes it much easier to add on the extensions. For example, if I wanted to construct a C Major 9 chord, I simply add in the ninth (the d note) and that's that.

The beautiful thing about the open position chord structure is that it's like a skeleton. It spreads your fingers out over 2 octaves and "opens up" the chord so adding in notes is easy!

Learn to Play the Piano Fast With This Cool Technique!

h ... the piano. So many want to learn how to play it. Yet all too often, lessons stop short. All that is about to change. You see, most people think they have learn note reading before they can make music on the piano.

But not only is note reading unnecessary, it's also a hindrance when it comes to being creative at the piano.

Here's a technique that will help you learn to play the piano fast! And it won't take you years, months, or even weeks. We're talking hours here - if that.

The technique I'm referring to is something called the open position chord. And with it, you'll be able to actually create your own unique music very, very quickly.

Let's take a look at how this is possible.

First, the open position chord uses both hands right away to create a nice modern sound at the piano. The chord is split between hands. The chord itself consists of six notes. You can see an example of this in the lesson, "Reflections in Water," available at quiescencemusic.com.

Second, as I mentioned earlier, it's a modern sounding chord. Most teachers start their students out with triads. There's nothing wrong with the humble triad. But why begin there, when you can work with a chord position that gives so much for so little effort.

For example, just by fingering an open position chord, you can make music. How is this possible? Because of the wide note spread. In fact, the open position chord takes up more than two octaves of the piano keyboard! With this much space, all you really have to do is play around with it and music comes out.

No one can adequately describe what the open position chord is. You have to experience it for yourself.

Left Hand Patterns for New Age Piano

Patterns. That's an interesting word and one that applies well to music. There are patterns everywhere in music. Repeating patterns, note patterns, chord patterns etc.

For New Age piano playing, a pattern that comes up frequently is a crossover technique for the left hand. The left plays a repeating pattern that uses more than an octave of the keyboard while the right plays melody notes, chords, etc.

For example, in the lesson, "Ocean Pacific," we have four chords to play with and the technique with which to play them - a repeating crossover pattern.

What is so great about this is that you have an aural background over which you may freely improvise your melodies. In essence, what is created is a repeating loop. This loop can also be looked at as a section of music. When you start thinking in sections, you'll be doing what composers do.

This pattern for the left hand is used frequently in New Age piano playing because you can create sections of music very quickly and easily. And it's attractive because it gives you the New Age sound quickly too!

How many patterns are there? An infinite amount. In fact, there are so many that it may be impossible to create them all. That's why music is so limitless. Experiment with your own patterns and you'll see how easy creating in the New Age style can be!

Left Hand Ostinato Patterns and Why They're Perfect for Piano Improvisation!

If you're a newbie to piano improvisation, you may be wondering what the best way to start out is. And while there are numerous ways to begin improvising on the piano, the ostinato technique is one of the easiest. Why? Because, once you have the pattern down in your left hand, your right hand can improvise melody freely.

Take a look at the lesson, "December Twilight."

Here we have a left hand ostinato pattern going on while the right improvises melody. The left hand plays a few bass notes - then two chords - A Major and D Major.

The great thing about this pattern is that it gives you a harmonic backdrop over which you improvise your own melody in the key of A Major. Plus, once your left hand is out of the way so to speak, you can focus your attention on the right and begin to improvise a melody.

Another lesson that uses this technique to good advantage is "Winter Scene." Here we have a different ostinato pattern going on. "Winter Scene" uses the modal scale of D dorian and just two chords from this scale.

The chords are played closer together so this gives us a completely different sound - but the technique is the same... that is, you are playing a left hand pattern while your right hand improvises melody.

Some students wonder about this technique. In fact, I've had one student tell me he gets bored with this. But the reason we play this kind of improvisation in the first place is to **enter into the flow of creativity easily.** This "exercise" allows you to forget about technique and which chords to play and literally forces you to improvise.

Of course, if we wanted to create a complete piece of music using this technique we could. Just look at George Winston's lovely piece, "Thanksgiving" and you'll see what I mean.

Modal Improvisation - An Easy Way To Get Started!

Most people really only know about or have heard of the major and minor scales. But did you know that there are thousands of other scales available to play?

Now don't worry. I'm not saying you should learn them or even know about all of them. Just a few of the more common ones used in New Age and Jazz music. Some of the scales I'm most fond of come from something called the "church modes."

They're called such because they were named and used back in Bach's time. And guess what? **They're still used today!**

For example, the lesson, "Cirrus," (you can hear this lesson at quiescencemusic.com - just scroll down and you'll see the play button) is a modern improvisation based on the Dorian mode. The Dorian mode is easy to construct because it's all on the white keys. To get it, just play the C major scale but instead of starting on C, you start and end on D.

You see, what this does is change the arrangement of

tones in the scale. A major scale has a major third and a major seventh in it. The D dorian scale has a minor third and a minor seventh making it a minor scale.

THE NUMERICAL RELATIONSHIP BETWEEN NOTES

Knowing the numerical relationship between notes will help you understand all this better. You can do this by simple counting.

Now that the boring technical stuff is out of the way, we can learn how to use the modes to create with. There are seven modes each corresponding to the note they begin on. Here they are:

C ionian (major) D dorian (minor) E phrygian (minor) F lydian (major) G mixolydian (major) A aeolian (minor) and B locrian (diminished)

There they are. And to form them, all you have to do is start and end on the note each begins with. For instance, the lesson, "Cirrus," begins with a D minor 7 chord in the right hand. This anchors the sound of the piece. We then use a few chords from this mode to really get a different sound going.

Most of us are familiar with the C major scale and its corresponding chords. Contemporary pianists/composers sometimes use the modes to mix things up and to create "new" sounds. I say "new" but they're really not new at all.

To get creative with the modes, pick one to play in. Write out all the chords that are in the mode, i.e. for the D dorian mode we have: D minor 7, E minor 7, F major 7, G 7, A minor 7, B diminished 7, A minor 7 and finally D minor 7 again.

Once you know the chords (again, all of the above are easily played on the white keys) you can start using them in your own improvisations!

More Right Hand Techniques For New Age Piano

What can you do on the piano? Answer? A lot! In fact, there are so many ways to hit notes it can get crazy.

One technique that's used by many New Age piano players is the right-hand crossover. Here the right hand **reaches over the left** to hit bass notes or chords. This adds a very rich and full sound to your playing.

Take lesson #7, "Caverns," for example. Here we have an opportunity to practice this technique. The left hand plays a simple ostinato pattern near the middle of the keyboard while the right plays bass and melody notes.

The beautiful thing about this technique is that it actually sounds like more than one piano! The left hand fills up the middle range while the right comes in with melody notes further up the keyboard. And then, when the player feels like it, bass notes are added in.

To master this technique, it's a good idea to begin with something very simple in the left hand. That's why in "Caverns," I have students play a very simple ostinato pattern. Once this is "down" it's quite easy to improvise melody and add in those booming bass notes. Another great thing about this technique is that it really allows you to get into improvisation.

It literally forces you to be in the moment. When you have so much going on with both hands the thinking mind can't catch up and this is perfect because you can now focus on expressing what you feel instead of thinking about whether what's coming out of you is good enough.

More Right-Hand Techniques for Piano Players

Most students new to piano playing really want to know what to do with the left hand. They think the left hand holds the secret to great improvisations and music. While it's true that the left hand has usually been the captain of the piano ship when it comes to setting arrangements, the right can also join in.

The right hand is where most of us create our melodies. It's considered easier than the workhorse part that the left has to do with creating arpeggios, ostinatos and the like. But, we can also use the right hand to create arpeggios and ostinato patterns.

For example, in the lesson, "April Rain," the right hand plays closed position seventh chords as arpeggios while the right plays bass notes as melody. This is not a new technique by far but it's not usually used in New Age piano playing.

And like any other technique, it takes a while before you feel comfortable enough to play a left-hand melody using bass notes. The piano is such a versatile instrument because unlike many other instruments, the notes are all laid out for you. You can switch hands, criss-cross hands, and do many other things with a piano keyboard that you just can't do with an instrument like a saxophone or even a guitar!

New Age Piano Playing and the Sustain Pedal

There are three pedals on most pianos. The one on the left dampens the strings and makes the sound come out softer. The one in the middle - I have no idea what that one does, but the one on the right - the sustain pedal - this one is the pedal I have my foot on when I play the piano.

I like to let the tones ring out, but if I keep the sustain pedal depressed for too long, the music turns into a mud puddle with hundreds of overtones coming out everywhere. Don't let anyone tell you that there is a proper way to pedal the piano.

Each style of music uses the sustain pedal differently. New age music, fortunately for us, is much more liberal with its use. Why? Because we usually throw the pedal "rules" out the window. The key to pedaling is to listen for the sound YOU WANT then pedal accordingly.

How do you think the great pianists and composers of the past did it? Do you think they asked themselves, "Well, maybe I should pedal here?" Of course not. They put pedal marks down where they themselves used it in a piece. You should do the same.

There's nothing like the ringing sound of overtones you get when you let the notes hang in mid-air. In fact, this is one of the charms of the piano - that mysterious echo barely discernible to the untrained ear, but there nevertheless providing warmth and realism to the music.

It's all accomplished through the use of the sustain pedal. When you want your music to breathe, use it. Experiment with it. Don't be afraid to keep it depressed for as long as you want to.

New Age Piano Techniques: Creative and Easy!

Every style of piano playing has its share of tricks and techniques. New Age piano is no different. The New Age piano style has 3 main techniques that are used over and over. These are the ostinato technique, the crossover technique or arpeggio, and the broken chord technique.

The Ostinato technique - A Repeating Pattern

You've probably heard this technique numerous times and may or may not have knows what it was. Ostinato simply means repeating pattern or obstinate pattern and that's exactly what it is. For example, in New Age pianist George Winston's piece, "Rain," we have a left hand pattern that uses over an octave of the keyboard to create a beautiful aural background over which a melody is improvised.

This technique is a very quick and easy way to create New Age piano pieces. The ostinato is played over and over while the right hand is able to "mix it up" and create change with the melody line. Of course, you can change the ostinato pattern as well as Winston does. With just a few small note changes, freshness is maintained and the piece moves listener attention forward. The author's one lesson piece, "Rainforest," does the same thing. Two chords are used in the left hand while the right improvises a melody.

The Crossover Technique - Arpeggios Up and Down

This technique is used everywhere in New Age piano and elsewhere. Usually spanning an octave or more, the pianist uses the left hand (mostly) to create a cascading pattern of notes that can ascend or descend or both depending on how it's played. Another good example of this technique is used in George Winston's piece, "Thanksgiving." Here he uses a few chords in the left hand broken up into arpeggios and creates a nice harmonic "loop" with them. Then the right hand improvises a melody and the piece is created. Very easy and quite nice as well.

The author's lesson piece, "Morning Mist," uses a few chords along with the crossover technique as well. First you learn how to play the left hand crossover, then you slowly add in a melody of your own. Creative? Yes! And easy as well!

The Broken Chord Technique - Both Hands In Play

Here we have a technique that sounds a lot more complicated than it really is. Both hands are used to create music with. The hands are placed on a chord and that chord is broken up.

For instance, the lesson, "Reflections in Water," uses broken chord technique along with open position chords to create a very nice "New Age" sound! Beginners who listen to this piece won't have a clue as to how it's accomplished but once you learn how to play the open position chord, insight will follow and you'll begin to see just how easy creating in the New Age style can be!

Open Position Piano Chords - Perfect for the New Age Style

The Open Position Chord (OPC) allows you to create a vented sound. A sound that is open, literally, as opposed to the closed triads taught in most course books.

The OPC covers more than two octaves of the keyboard

allowing you to create without moving the hands around too much. Perfect for the beginner and advanced player. New Age music in particular has an open quality that is created in a number of ways.

The first way is by the chord choices used. Most of this music is in a Major Key. The sound is pleasant without any dissonant tones.

The second way is how the chord is played or voiced. The OPC voicing gives you the ability to separate the chord into three different parts; low end or bass note, middle notes, and high or melody notes. With this configuration you are able to make more music than if you were just playing a triad in your left hand and playing melody in your right.

It also allows you to play in counterpoint. When you are improvising with the OPC, your fingers will automatically begin to create a countermelody. How? Because you already have six tones underneath your fingers with which to begin. Just by moving your fingers over the keys in different rhythms, you begin to have harmony with melody.

It allows you to play piano with both hands together right away. This is entirely different than the way most pianists learn how to finger a chord. They are usually taught triads first, fingered in the left hand then in the right and finally both hands together. Is this music making? Of course not.

The Open Position Chord allows you to use both hands together to create solid chords, arpeggios - pretty much anything you can imagine. This chord structure allows the complete beginner to sound like a pro faster than any other approach. Why? Because you are already using seventh chords - the foundation sound for most modern music today. It's used in jazz and contemporary instrumental music about 90% of the time. After you begin to play the OPC as a seventh chord, there's no end to the possibilities.

Perfect Pitch:
Is it Really Necessary?

What is perfect pitch? It's when tones can be identified when heard. For example, if I play a G note on the piano and someone can name that note correctly, they are considered to have perfect pitch.

Is perfect pitch necessary in order to play and create music? NOT AT ALL!

You don't even have to know what notes you're playing in order to make music. Having perfect pitch is not the great asset some would have you believe it is. Yet many students want to acquire this skill.

Let's see what having perfect pitch can actually do for you. It can let you know what key you're playing in. Nice, but we have key signatures that make this task obsolete. Most musicians are already aware of the key they're playing in before they sit down to play. Even jazz musicians determine key before playing. True, they may deviate from the original key but having perfect pitch is not required for this.

You can tell what note you're playing when you play it. So what! A typist knows what letter they're typing when then input it into the keyboard but knowing what the letter is doesn't make for good writing.

Having perfect pitch is not really a skill anyone should waste their time learning. If you do have it (and some people are born with this ability), then great. If you don't, please save your time and energy and don't be sold on the idea that knowing what note you're playing will make you a great musician. It won't. It will make you aware of what note you're playing and that's that. Nice for the ego. Unnecessary for making music... no matter what instrument you play.

Piano Chord Changes and How to Chart Them Out

As much as I like to just "fool around" on the piano, there comes a time when I want to remember or capture what I've been doing. But what's an easy way to do this you ask? I'll tell you. By charting out your chord changes on a piece of paper, you'll remember the harmonic background easier. Here's how.

First, get a sheet of paper. Any paper will do. It doesn't have to be lined or ruled and it doesn't have to be music paper. Next draw out 8-bars. I usually just draw 4 bars, skip down some and then draw another 4-bars. This is your chord chart! It doesn't have to be more complicated than this. In fact, this quick sketch method will serve you well when inspiration is running high and you want to very quickly jot down your chord changes.

You can do it anywhere! On a napkin, on a piece of paper in your purse or wallet. In fact, I've actually used ATM receipts to jot down chord changes on.

After you draw out 8-bars, you know have a template to use. You simply write your chord symbols on top. The chord changes may last for 1 bar, 2 bars... whatever. Eight bar frameworks are excellent to work in because they give you your first section of music! Plus, it's a nice space of time to work in. In fact, you could use just 2 chords and fill out the 8-bars, i.e., C Major for the first 4 bars and F Major for the next 4.

After you fill up this 8-bar space, you have basically captured the harmony aspect. But, you'll probably want to jot down the first 2-bars of melody as well. This will really help you remember what you are creating. You might also want to sketch out the arrangement of your chord changes. For example, if you are playing arpeggios in the left hand, indicate the pattern by writing it in for 2-bars.

Well, there you have it, my quick sketch method for creating chord changes.

Piano Chord Charts and How to Use Them

Piano chord charts are used to help you keep track of chord changes. And the cool thing about them is that you can use them for improvisation and composition. Here's how.

Let's say you have an 8-bar phrase to play. There are no chord symbols yet so you don't know what chords you'll be playing. You just have 8-bars in front of you. The first thing you need to know is the time signature. For our purposes here, we'll keep it simple and use 3/4 or 4/4 time.

Now let's select 4/4 time for our 8-bar phrase. Now we know the meter but what about the chords? Here's where we can jot down chord progressions for either improvisation or composition. For example, you may want to begin something in the Key of F Major. Having made that decision, you know that you have six chords to use right away. These are F Major, G minor, A minor. B flat Major, C 7, and D minor.

All that's left to do now is begin your piece in the Key of F Major. We usually start with the F Major chord itself so you now know that your first bar or 2 will be the F Major chord. But now a problem arises - how do you fill up the rest of the space? By using an 8-bar phrase to begin with, you don't have to worry about filling up a lot of space and taking forever to complete a section of music.

For instance, let's suppose we want to chart out an 8-bar phrase for improvisation purposes. We know what chords we will be working with. Now it's just a matter of fooling around on the piano and playing with the chord choices. You may want to place a chord change at every two measures. You can even use two chords for the entire 8-bar phrase such as F Major and B flat Major.

The whole point of the piano chord charts is to have a tool that will help you navigate what chords to play and when to change chords.

Piano Chords and New Age Music

There are basically two ways you can compose a piece of music. The first and most traditional way is to write out the melody and then harmonize it. Some call this working from the top (as opposed to the chords on the bottom.) The second approach is where you create some kind of rhythmic harmonic pattern and improvise (or compose) the melody on top. Which one is best for New Age music?

The answer is neither approach. Each has its own merits and own special benefits. For example, if you start with a pattern in your left hand and improvise a melody with your right, you are doing what most new age composers/improvisers do. This is what George Winston does most of the time. He has chords he sets to a certain rhythm and does his thing with that amazing right hand of his.

This is the style that I have been playing, but I've recently lost interest in it. Not because it isn't good but because I don't feel like playing that way anymore. Currently I'm leaning towards a softer sound that comes from leading with the melody first. What I do is get the first 2-bars down and then improvise the rest till I fill up eight measures. This way I can vary the chords and patterns without it sounding very repetitive (minimalism). It's actually another style. You can call it melodic while the other one (Harmony approach) is more textural. IT ALL DEPENDS ON YOUR MOOD!

Don't let one style freeze you into something where you can't maneuver artistically! Remember that your feeling must come first. Everything else is secondary. Let your feeling lead you and your creation will be truly inspired, however, if you try to mold what you have to say into a specific style, the result may be less than satisfactory.

Piano Improvisation Techniques: Creating The Arpeggio

A h… the arpeggio. A miracle of cascading notes that produces a beautiful sound on the piano. To most it's a mystery how it's created. But to those who understand chords, it's just a matter of practicing until the pattern is mastered.

Now, the arpeggio can be used either in the right or left hand (or both together) but it's usually the left hand that takes up this amazing technique. Let's look at how one might use an extended arpeggio pattern to create an improvisation.

The first thing you need to know about most left-hand arpeggios is that they usually start below the middle of the keyboard. **Most pianists begin their run below middle C** and there's a good reason for this - bass notes!

Those thunderous resonant bass sounds that reverberate in the body are hit and the piano comes alive!

Now, you have to be careful here because if you hit too many bass notes together the effect can end up sounding "muddy." That is, you won't be able to differentiate the notes and you'll end up having sonic sludge. But, if you spread out the first few notes this won't happen. That's why **the open position chord is perfect to begin your left hand arpeggio.** For example, let's say you want to play a C Major 9 arpeggio.

Of course, you'll begin with the C note (which is also the root note.) Now, we could play the third (e) but if we do, chances are we'll end up with that "muddy" effect. No, A better way is to play the fifth followed by either the octave or the seventh tone.

What I like to do is play a pattern that looks like this: 1-5-8-9-3 -which means I'm playing these notes: c-g-c-d-e. This pattern produces a beautiful "new age" sound and is used frequently in New Age piano playing.

For example, look at the lesson, "Coming Home." Here we play an extended arpeggio in the left hand and use over 2 octaves of the keyboard. It's quite an exercise and is a good one to get your left hand moving!

Piano Instruction - It Doesn't Have to be a Chore for You!

You want to learn piano. There are many methods of piano instruction available on the market today. Let's look at what's out there.

Method 1 - Note Reading and the Classical Repertoire

Not a bad choice if you love the classics and want to spend your time learning how to note read. This option is what most piano students choose, yet I don't understand why. After all, you might as well throw creativity out the door. You're playing other people's music, for crying out loud!

Method 2 - Chord Understanding and Improvisation

Here's where the fun really begins! Learning how to use chords to create your own music is a world apart from note reading and will give you more joy then most any other method. Why? Because you are actively involved in the music making process! Why do you think so many guitar players can just pick up their instrument and play? It's because they learn chords first. Note reading is not emphasized as much for the guitar player.

So, where can you find this kind of piano instruction? There are many teachers who know how to play using the chord-based approach but can't teach this method. A teacher should do more than just give you the techniques and send you on your way. A good teacher will help you trust yourself and the music you play and will act as a mentor, guiding you to your desired goals.

Piano Keyboards and How to Use Them

When most people look at a piano keyboard, they see a sea of black and white keys. They can't understand how someone can sit down at this confusing combination of notes and create music.

Of course they can't! They haven't learned how to look at the piano keyboard in such a way that it all makes sense. All they really need to do is understand how to see it like the pros do. And pros see the piano keyboard as scales and chords.

All you really need to know to start out is to learn chords and that's it. Just think of the guitar player as an analogy. They begin to make sense of their instrument rather quickly. Why? Because they are taught chords from the beginning. They learn to play the three most important chords in any key right away and begin to make music. They begin to look at the fretboard as more advanced players do - as a way to produce music through chords.

They then learn how to finger a scale and the guitar fretboard no longer seems a mystery but an acoustic terrain to be mastered.

The same principles apply to the piano. Once you have a few chords under your belt and can play the scale (much simpler for pianists than guitarists) you will begin to see the piano keyboard in a new way.

For example, I'm a big fan of something called the open position chord. It covers more than two octaves of the piano keyboard and gives the beginning player a modern sound right away. Once students begin playing it, they soon discover that they can quickly make music just like their guitar playing counterparts!

Piano Lessons for the Creatively Challenged!

A re you a creative klutz? Does the thought of playing piano not only frighten but also intimidate you? If so, there's a solution. It's called the open position piano chord and with it, you'll be able to create your own music within one hour, guaranteed! Here's how.

Chords are used to make music at the piano. The same way a guitar player can pick up the guitar, strum a few chords and make music, so too can the pianist. The problem is, note reading is what has been usually taught while creativity with chords is relegated to background status. The open position piano chord is a unique chord structure that utilizes both hands right away to create a modern sounding chord that is used in today's contemporary music.

You don't need years of theory in order to play it and you don't need to understand harmony. All you need to do is practice this chord at the piano and within minutes, you'll be able to improvise your own unique music. For example, in the lesson, "Reflections in Water," (available quiescence-music.com) you have four chords from the key of C Major to work with. And four chords are more than enough to begin creating your own music.

We finger the first chord, C Major 7 and notice that our hands are used to their maximum capacity. That is, this chord structure really stretches your hands allowing you to cover more than two octaves (16 keys). It really is quite amazing! It will take a little while to get used to, but once the chord position is mastered, a whole new world of sound awaits you.

Many piano courses begin students with triads. There is nothing wrong with triads. They've been used for centuries. The problem is that the sound is not something most students equate with "modern" sounding styles, i.e. New Age, Jazz. The open position piano chord allows you to create a modern sound right away and is perfect for the creatively challenged beginning piano student!

Piano Music - How to Begin and End a Piece

How do you begin a piece of music? That's a question I'm often asked. The answer I usually give is that you begin as soon as you start playing. If you're trying to "compose" something, the piece begins the moment it has energy and is something you want to capture. If it's an improvisation, the piece begins the moment you set your fingers on the keys and hit the first note. It's like free flow writing and writing a chapter to a novel.

The writer can both improvise and enjoy the process or can structure the ideas more - or, as I like to do, combine both procedures into one. I start out by improvising – always. Then, if I want to memorialize a musical idea, I write down the first two bars of melody along with the chord(s) I'm playing. I throw this on a chart and voila - the idea remains fresh until I want to either expand on it, or ignore it completely.

If the idea is a rhythm pattern I write down (Left hand = whatever the pattern is) so I can remember it later. I never stop improvising though because that would stop the flow and who knows what could come out of it. Don't forget that an improvisation is a piece of music in and of itself. There is really no need to impose structure on something as beautiful and organic as spontaneous expression. In fact, these spur of the moment fantasies are often more inspiring than any contrived composition. There is something more alive to them because there IS more life to them.

Endings pose another problem, namely the problem of when to stop playing. For improvisation, the answer is when energy (inspiration) starts to wane down. That's a good time to bring your music to an end. You'll know when this is happening when you become bored. That's the sign it's time to stop.

Composition is a different story. The form of the piece already dictates when you should stop. For example, an ABA form tells you to play the A section once or twice, go to B, back to A, then bring the piece to an end. The amount of repetition and contrast is a personal decision but the form establishes both beginning and ending. It's a nice safe way to say that yes, I have a piece of music here. Improvisations can have form as well. The big difference is that you don't consciously think about putting the music into a predefined shape.

But for some unknown reason, most improvisations do have symmetry - that is they take on a form of their own. I don't know if this is because of human beings innate rhythm (heartbeat) or what.

Even Zen flute music, which may be the most freely inspired improvisation style around has some structure. You can hear it in the phrases. Beginnings and endings. Don't worry too much about them. What's important is where you are emotionally while you play. Become aware of that and all your problems are solved.

Piano Notes - How To Achieve Hand Independence on the Piano

"I'm losing the left hand," cried one piano student. "Every time I try to add in my right hand, the left stops!" exclaims another.

These are common complaints for students who wish to learn hand independence. And for most, this is a big problem. They want to play the piano with both hands playing different parts. But the main reason most piano students have problems with this is because they try to play too fast!

Hand independence is one area that takes some time (not too much time) but some time to achieve. And this too depends on how complicated the hands tasks are.

START OUT GOING SLOW!

For example, in the lesson, "Winter Scene," we have a left hand ostinato pattern going while the right hand improvises a melody. This lesson uses just two chords in closed position. By giving you only two chords, I conveniently limit the left hand's ability to go all over the place.

You start out by going slow and easy until the left hand is so automatic that you can play the pattern while talking to someone. In fact, you should be able to keep the left hand going while doing anything else. That's how automatic it can become with a little practice. Then you add in the right hand to improvise a melody.

Here is where most students mess up. Why? Because they try to play something too complicated or sophisticated in the right hand. Here's the answer - go as slow as you need to maintain the left hand! There's no need to rush. If all you can play is one note, then play that note. This isn't to say that you shouldn't play around with the possibilities and experiment with your right hand. It is to say that if you're a speed demon here, you're defeating your own purpose.

When a simple ostinato pattern becomes second nature, you can get more sophisticated in the left hand. For instance, in lesson 60, "Sea Caves," we use over an octave in the left hand while the right plays sixth notes and single note runs.

Hand independence is something you can achieve - but you must have patience. Slow and steady wins the race here.

Piano Playing Tips for
The Creatively Impaired

Lets face it... you're not one to just sit down at the piano and have beautiful music come up. No. You're more like someone who struggles just to get one original note out. It doesn't have to be that way. In fact, playing piano can be a joy. Here are three piano playing tips to help you loosen up and get into a creative space.

Piano Playing Tip #1: You Know Enough to Begin Now

Don't wait until you think you're ready. Begin now and enjoy the feeling of creating your own music. You know enough to begin. Don't think so? What do you really need to know? A few chords and how to play them - THAT'S' IT! You don't need to spend months or years in school learning theory. Theory is good to know and can come later. For example, I know how to construct a D minor 9 chord easily but I wish I knew what to do with it long before I learned how to make it.

The way to begin is to begin easy. Start by learning a few chords. Then use them by improvising. The way to make music as you go is to stay in the present. If you even think of anything but the music making you won't be able to get as much enjoyment out of your playing. The way to stay in the present is to play. Play like children play - with an open mind and open heart. Not expecting anything but glad for what happens - spontaneously. Do you think a child questions whether she knows enough to begin painting? Of course not. Yet we as adults place all kinds of limits on ourselves.

Piano Playing Tip #2: You Can Learn to Improvise and Create Your Own Music

Do you think you need to be in school for years to acquire improvisational skills? If you do, you're not alone. Most people share this belief. Practice is what will give you the skill to create spontaneously. More specifically, practice without judgment will really get you there fast. You grow in proportion to the amount of time you spend playing the piano. You learn then come upon times when growth slows down. This does not mean that growth has stopped. It only means you are changing internally - readying yourself for the next new spurt.

Piano Playing Tip #3: No One Knows Everything

I wish I really believed this one before I got started playing piano. I really believed that you had to learn a lot to make music. The truth of the matter is even when I knew "sophisticated" chords and chord voicing, I still was blocked! When I started playing simply, using just a few chords, I could easily improvise and forget myself at the piano. What a difference in approach! I self-judged myself right into not being able to play. I say "play" because this is what improvisation is. I believed that it was more important that I sound good to others than feel good about what I was doing at the piano. It was a crucial error on my part and one that's taken a long time to rectify.

Gaining others approval can kill the spirit and destroy the ability to create because you will never be good enough! You must please yourself first - then share the music with others. To know everything is to know nothing. There are no good musicians or bad musicians. There is only you and the music. Is it good or bad? Who cares! What's important is your feeling and not the product that comes out.

Piano Tabs - Who Needs Them?

As a piano player you have three choices available to you for learning; these are, note reading, piano tabs, and chord-based approach.

Most students who use piano tabs do so because they want to avoid the note reading approach altogether. They just want to be able to quickly play their favorite tunes without having to invest a substantial amount of time learning musical notation. These same students would be able to learn the piano even quicker if they learned a chord-based approach first. Here's why.

It's Quick. Guitar players know this. They don't spend months learning note reading but dive into chord playing right away. In fact, guitarists may be the only musicians who do this on a regular basis - hence the popularity of this instrument. Within just a few minutes, they have learned their first chord and are off enjoying music. Pianists can also learn this approach but usually don't because they either don't know about it, or think it's too difficult. They think they must learn sophisticated jazz voicing or some other complicated harmony first. Nope. A piano player can quickly create music as fast as the guitarist and all it takes is just a rudimentary knowledge of a few chords.

It's Easy. How hard is it to place your fingers on a chord? It's actually easier for the pianist to do this than the guitar player. There are no steel strings to hurt the fingers. No need to press down on the fret board. Just place your fingers on a chord, depress the keys, and voila - a piano chord. In fact, you can be playing and creating modern sounding music much easier than the guitar player, especially if you use the open position chord. Here we have a modern sound that uses both hands to full capacity. And it's easy!

Don't waste your time learning piano tablature. Learn chords instead. That way, you'll be able to sound more professional in less time than practically any other method!

Piano for the Fun of It: Creating with the Open Position Chord

You're a fan of the piano. You like the way it looks and sounds but you're too afraid to approach the task of learning how to play it.

You're not alone! Literally millions of people would love to learn this instrument but don't because they're intimidated by the learning curve.

But fear no more! Your learning curve just got a lot

shorter thanks to the Open Position Chord! This versatile chord structure allows the beginning piano student to sound like a pro faster than any other method I know of! Why? Because it allows you to play a modern sounding chord with both hands right away.

There's no note reading or piano tabs to concern yourself with here for by learning how to play this unique chord structure, you can start to create your own unique music! The Open Position Chord covers more than two octaves of the piano keyboard. The hands are used to maximum capacity to create a rich, full sounding chord that contemporary pianists use today.

We start by learning all the Open Position Chords in the key of C. There are seven of them, but six are used most frequently. They are C Major 7, D minor 7, E minor 7, F Major 7, G 7, A minor 7, and B half-diminished 7. This last chord is almost the same as G 7 and is rarely used in most music today.

We take this six-note chord structure beginning with C Major 7 and move it up the scale one note at a time creating the chords you see named above. For example, in the lesson, "Reflections in Water," (available at quiescencemusic.com) we use 4 of these chords to create a unique little improvisation. Just knowing the chords and the C Major scale is enough material for the complete beginner to begin making music.

Play Chord Piano Fast With This Easy To Use Technique!

Techniques. Some of them are more useful than others, especially when it comes to piano playing. What you're about to learn is a special way of forming chords at the keyboard that will have you playing chord piano in no time.

It's called **the open position chord** and it's exactly what its name implies - a chord structure that covers more than two octaves of the keyboard and uses both hands right away.

The open position chord (or OPC for short) is not an easy chord position to master at first, but once you get it in your hands, you'll be well on your way to playing chord piano.

Let's take a look at how we might go about learning this new technique. Take a look at my free piano lesson, "Reflections in Water." Here we have four open position chords in the key of C major. You'll notice the play button along with keyboard diagrams. Listen to the OPC and notice the sound. It's quite modern isn't it?

Now take a look at the keyboard diagrams and familiarize yourself with this chord. Once you get a feel for this chord structure you're left with how to use it. **This is the fun part!** What I did in the lesson, "Reflections in Water," is simply to play the OPC's and improvise melody using notes from the C Major scale. That's it! That's all that's required to create your own unique music.

You see, learning the OPC makes it all the easier. Because you have such a wide note spread between your fingers, it allows you to make "more" music, so to speak, than if you were to use triads or closed position chords.

Even the audio part where I just play the chords is musical. Many of you want to learn how to play piano using chords. I suggest starting with the OPC because it gives you instant satisfaction on the keyboard!

Play Chord Piano Now - Even If You Don't Know Major from Minor!

D o you know why people think guitar is easier to learn than piano? It's because they know that all that is required to get music from a guitar is to finger a chord. And that in itself is quite easily accomplished.

Mention the word "piano" though and fear leaps up in the throats of prospective students. Where to begin? So much to learn? So many notes? You see, what scares so many students is that sea of shiny black and white that at first - looks so mysterious. After all, how DO you make music with all of these notes?

That's a great question. And I have the answer for you. You make sense of piano notes the same way you make sense of the guitar - **by learning chords!**

But not just any chord. Not the triad, even though most music teachers start you off learning this basic chord structure. A great way to learn and understand keyboard harmony is to learn something called the open position chord.

This chord structure uses both hands to create a modern sound right off the bat! And once you learn the six basic chords in the key of C Major, you'll begin to see the keyboard in a whole new way. You'll start to see that music is made from chords and melody and that it does not require more than learning a few basic chords to start.

For example, in the lesson, "Peaceful Pond," you play a few open position chords in the key of E flat Major to create music with. You play within one key and keep things simple.

Another problem beginning students have is they think they have to learn sophisticated chord voicing and patterns before they begin creating music. This is really a way to avoid jumping in the improvisational waters so to speak. The best way to start is to start easy. Then, when keyboard harmony is understood, new voicing and patterns emerge.

To play chord piano now, learn the open position chord. You'll enjoy it!

Play New Age Piano Now With This Easy to Use Technique

New Age piano is a beautiful style of music that many use to relax and unwind. But did you know that it's also easy to create on your own? You don't need a lot of theory or background in music to start playing piano in the New Age style.

All you really need is to know a few chords and then jump in and play. Most teachers start students off with the humble triad. And while there's nothing wrong with this chord type, it's not very modern sounding.

In fact, triads have been used in music for over 300 years. They still are being used but if you want a more modern sound right away, I suggest you learn something called the "open position" chord. This chord structure allows you to use both hands right away to create a beautiful modern sound. And it's quite easy to learn.

For example, in the lesson, "Reflections in Water," (available at quiescencemusic.com) you have four chords to learn. And once these are under your fingers, you can start exploring with music. You can actually begin improvising and creating your very own New Age piano music. I know this sounds too easy. But if you take a look at the video lesson, you'll see me demonstrating it. First, you learn how to play the open position chords. Then you use these same chords to create with.

If you really want to play New Age piano now, I highly recommend the open position chord.

Play Piano By Ear In Less Than One Hour!

So, you want to learn how to play piano by ear. You think this skill is reserved for those with "special" talent. You're wrong about that!

What does it mean to play by ear? Simply, the musician understands the fundamentals of diatonic harmony. To understand this, you just need to know a little about chords.

For example, in the key of C Major we have seven chords. These are: C Major, D minor, E minor, F Major G Major, A minor and B half-diminished.

Notice that these chords are lined up in order and that they are triads. Most harmonic theory in the western world gives a number to these chords using roman numerals. Simply put, we can call the C Major chord 1, the D minor chord 2, and so on. You see how it works.

FAMILIARIZE YOURSELF WITH THESE CHORDS!

Once you familiarize yourself with these chords, you get to learn something that most composers have known for centuries and that is <u>certain chord progressions have tension</u> and others don't.

To play piano by ear, you need to learn the most frequently used chord progression and that is the 1-4-5 progression. To put it into chord terms, it's simply the C Major chord followed by the F Major chord and then the G Major chord.

Knowing these three chords will help you play piano by ear guaranteed. How? Because these chords are used in almost ALL the music here in the West! Which is to say, most pop songs use them and many, many classical compositions use them. They are the bedrock of modern western harmonic theory.

You may be asking yourself why these chords are so important. You see it all has to do with the scale! When you play a C Major scale, you are defining the chords that can come from it. When we construct triads using this scale, the chords that are generated give a certain sound. Composers discovered that the most tension exists between the 1 and the 5 chords.

The early composers prized tension because it meant that they could control how to build up to climax and how to release as well.

To play the piano by ear, learn these three chords in ALL keys. You'll soon get the secret!

Right Hand Techniques for New Age Piano

Recently, I had a student ask me to offer some techniques for using the right hand. Usually, it's the left hand that causes the most difficulty but I had to think about it because up till then, I really did not have any "techniques" for the right hand.

I thought about it and tried to think about what I do as far as improvising with the right hand goes. Basically there are really only a few things you can do. You can:

Play single note runs -this is where you just play one note at a time

Play arpeggios -broken chords up and down the keyboard

Play chords -using thirds or sixths or any combination of the chord-scale relationship

Different genres of music use the above techniques in different ways. New Age piano usually relies on a softer sound although there is a "minimalist" style that uses hard sounding chords in the right hand a la George Winston.

You see, the problem is that you have to know the numerical relationship between the root note and the rest of the notes that make up the chord to "know what you're doing" on the keyboard.

A book I highly recommend, although it may not be on the market anymore, is Alan Swain's *Four-way Keyboard System*. It's not an easy instruction book, but it is one of the best for how chords are constructed -thus allowing you to know when you are playing thirds or fourths and so on. Not necessary for making music, but nice to know anyway.

The Crossover Technique and How to Use It

The piano is an amazing instrument. So many notes, so many keys! That's why the crossover or arpeggio technique is employed frequently. It allows the pianist to use much of the keyboard and the left hand.

The trick to using this technique is in the crossover itself. Usually, the left hand's initial position will span an octave and then the index or ring finger will be used to crossover the thumb to continue playing more notes of the chord.

A good example of this is the piece, "Thanksgiving," by George Winston. Here, a whole harmonic background is created by the left-hand crossover technique while the right improvises a melody line. And the results are a beautiful piece of music! Nothing complicated here. He just gets his left hand down using a few chords. This creates the backdrop for the entire piece -and the mood!

You too can create your own harmonic backgrounds. Once you learn how to do the crossover technique, you'll find it to be something you'll use over and over again. Why? Because of its capacity to use much of the keyboard and the beautiful sound you can get from it.

There are many variations to the crossover technique as well. In fact, you can actually use it to cover more than four octaves of the keyboard! You just keep crossing over with the left hand to cover as many notes as you wish. Another great example of this technique is the lesson, "Morning Mist!" Here we use four chords and a simple crossover technique to create a light ambiance. We keep playing these chords in the left hand while the right is free to improvise a melody and we have created a beautiful piece of music!

The One Piano Playing Technique That Makes Even Tone Deaf Students Sound Good!

When I first heard this technique applied over 15 years ago, I couldn't believe my ears. How could so much music be coming out of one piano? Turns out, what I was hearing was something called an "ostinato." Ostinato simply means repeating pattern and is used frequently in all kinds of music.

But it really shines for the New Age piano genre. Just listen to George Winston's piece, "Rain" to get an idea of what can be done with this technique. He uses a very large chunk of the keyboard to create a beautiful left hand ostinato pattern while the right hand improvises. And what music! You'd swear it couldn't be just one piano but it is!

Now, ostinatos can be used to create a staccato sound (as in the Winston piece, "Rain") or they can be used gently as in the lesson piece, "Winter Scene."

Here we use two chords to create a nice harmonic background. Once the left hand is set, so to speak, the right hand enters in with an improvised melody. And that's all that is required to create a full piece of music!

An ostinato pattern can use as much or as little of the keyboard as the player desires. In fact, if you just play a repeating bass note you've created an ostinato pattern. The lesson, "Winter Scene," uses suspended chords that are broken up. Winston's piece Rain actually uses a left-hand arpeggio pattern - yes, an arpeggio can be turned into an ostinato too!

Once we have the ostinato pattern, we can create a harmonic loop. We can chart out the chord changes on a piece of paper and notate our pattern for future use. Ostinatos are great because they quickly give you the entire background and mood of the piece. We then "paint" our melodies on top of this background to create our aural canvas!

The Only Piano Book You'll Ever Need

'll never forget the time I took my first piano class. It was at the Community College of Philadelphia in 1984. It was a group class with 20 or so electronic keyboards arranged around the room. We each received a class text book titled "*Class Piano*." No shocker there.

I opened up the book and saw that I would be learning how to read music and play triads. I also saw that I would be playing very simple classical pieces. Now, while I enjoyed this and learned how to play these easy pieces, it just didn't do it for me. It was because as I soon as I put the book down, I was dumbfounded! I didn't know what to do on the piano without the book!

I soon realized that I didn't want to become a professional note reader. No. I wanted to be able to sit down at the piano, place my fingers on a chord that called to me, and just play. I wanted to express myself at the piano in the same way visual artists are able to take pen and paper and artfully color their inner worlds. Why was this so difficult to do?

It was at this time that I started to look for new ways to play. I came upon a book that taught a modern chord position that could be used right away to make music. Amazing! No note reading. Just chords. And once I learned a few chords, I was able to create my own music. This open position chord structure allowed me to improvise music quite easily.

Another book influenced me as well. This one showed how to play chord progressions using 4, 8 and 16 bar phrases. With this chord charting technique, I could see that I could create my own pieces. It taught me the principles of repetition and contrast - the cornerstones to musical composition.

A few chords arranged for 8-bars is repeated two or more times giving you what is called an "A" section of music. Another few bars of different chord changes and the "B" section is produced. And all of this was taught within a very slim volume. Maybe 46 pages or so.

After a few years of working with this material, I synthesized both methods so beginning piano players can take a modern sounding chord and work with it within a set framework. The result is a method where students are able to improvise their own music right away!

The Open Position Piano Chord

Chords. They're amazing. There's no doubt about it. Especially when it comes to piano playing and the Open Position Chord. Here we can use both hands to create music with. The chord is broken up into its main elements and its voicing is spread out which gives it a nice open sound - the sound that's perfect for the New Age style.

To use the OPC requires little more than fingering the chord itself because once the chord is played, music comes out. All that's required now is to be able to experiment with the sounds and textures. It's absolutely critical that the thinking mind stops and feeling be allowed to come to the front.

This is possible by adopting an attitude of abeyance. Not being concerned with what's coming out of you.

For example in lesson 20, "Reflections in Water," I use the OPC to create a gentle mood. How? By first allowing myself to get in right brain mode, then letting my fingers do the walking! I know what the chords are, I know that I'll be using the OPC. I then let it all go and let my feeling lead me to where it wants to go and this always leads to the ideal music.

The Ostinato - What It Is and How to Use It

Ostinato means "repeating pattern" and is used frequently in all types of music. For New Age piano players, it provides a great way to lay down the background of the piece while the right hand improvises a melody!

For example, in the lesson, "Winter Scene," we have a repeating pattern going on in the left hand using two chords. And two chords are all that is needed to create a few minutes of music!

Interest is maintained by the right-hand melody. How long you could actually play this ostinato and maintain interest is a whole new topic but the secret to really keeping the improvisation going is to stay in the present and trust your intuition.

The music will naturally wind down when you start becoming bored or indifferent and/or no new material wants to come. Then the improvisation is over and the music has played itself out.

The good thing about using an ostinato to create is that it's quite easy to develop a harmonic background over which you can improvise your melodies. The bad thing is that it tends to stagnate over time. That's when you either stop playing, or introduce new material - something that adds contrast.

If you wanted, you could introduce another ostinato pattern, or go for something completely different, but you'd probably want to let your intuition guide you in this. You shouldn't try to come up with material but instead, just improvise and see what comes up. A completely different, and much more effective approach!

The Piano Keyboard and the Open Position Chord

Did you know that the piano keyboard is not used to its fullest potential? And that thousands of beginning piano students start out by playing a three-note triad that is as outdated as the dinosaur?

It's true. The piano keyboard is huge! Over 80 keys big. Why not come up with a chord structure that uses more keys? Why not indeed!

There is a chord structure called the Open Position chord

that uses more than two octaves of the keyboard. Both hands are called into play here to create a modern sounding seventh chord that is used frequently in pop, jazz, and new age music.

It's not an easy chord structure to learn right away, BUT once learned, **it allows you to sound like a professional pianist right away**! Why? Because of the way the chord is structured. It's easy to sound modern when the sound coming from the chord is. It's really a no-brainer and it's a shame that most piano teachers either never use it or have never heard of it.

I first came across it in a book titled "*The Four-Way Keyboard System*" by Alan Swain, a noted jazz pianist. As soon as I played this chord, I knew I had found something special. With it, I could create modern sounds immediately. And I could use it to improvise my own music – something I've always wanted to do.

Once I learned how to play this special chord structure, I learned how to move it up and down the piano keyboard thus learning how to use all 88 keys. It was thrilling to be able to do this. Why not use the piano keyboard to its fullest potential. Learn how to play the Open Position piano chord!

Breinigsville, PA USA
28 November 2010
250219BV00001B/15/P